FLAGSHIP HISTORYMAKERS

JFK & LBJ

DERRICK MURPHY

An imprint of HarperCollins*Publishers*

Dedication
To Neville on his retirement.

Published by HarperCollins*Publishers* Ltd
77–85 Fulham Palace Road
London
W6 8JB

Browse the complete Collins catalogue at
www.collinseducation.com

© HarperCollins*Publishers* Ltd 2004
First published 2004

ISBN 000 717323 7

British Library Cataloguing in Publication Data. A
catalogue record for this book is available from the
British Library.

Series commissioned by Graham Bradbury
Project management by Will Chuter
Edited by Hayley Willer
Book and cover design by Derek Lee
Map artwork by Richard Morris
Picture research by Celia Dearing
Index by Julie Rimington
Production by Sarah Robinson
Printed and bound by Printing Express Ltd.,
Hong Kong

ACKNOWLEDGEMENTS

The Publishers would like to thank the following
for permission to reproduce extracts from their
books:

Longman for an extract from *State and Society in
Twentieth-Century America*, by R. Harrison (1997).
University of Texas Press for an extract from 'The
War in Vietnam', by G.C. Herring, in *The Johnson
Years: Foreign Policy, the Great Society, and the
White House*, edited by Robert A. Divine (1981).

The Publishers would like to thank the following
for permission to reproduce pictures on these pages
(T=Top, B=Bottom, L=Left, R=Right, C=Centre):

© Corbis 57, © Bettmann/Corbis 12, 19, 24, 32, 34,
35, 41, 47, 48, 52B, 59, © Hulton-Deutsch
Collection/Corbis 9, 52C, © Wally McNamee/Corbis
52T; Getty Images/Hulton Archive 20;
Popperfoto.com 7.

Cover picture: © Bettmann/Corbis

Every effort has been made to contact the holders
of copyright material, but if any have been
inadvertently overlooked the Publishers will be
pleased to make the necessary arrangements at the
first opportunity.

You might also like to visit
www.harpercollins.co.uk
The book lovers' website

Contents

Why do historians differ?

THE purpose of the Flagship Historymakers series is to explore the main debates surrounding a number of key individuals in British, European and American History.

Each book begins with a chronology of the significant events in the lives of the particular individuals, and an outline of their careers. The book then examines in greater detail three of the most important and controversial issues in the lives of the individuals – issues which continue to attract differing views from historians, and which feature prominently in examination syllabuses in A-level History and beyond.

Each of these issue sections provides students with an overview of the main arguments put forward by historians. By posing key questions, these sections aim to help students to think through the areas of debate and to form their own judgements on the evidence. It is important, therefore, for students to understand why historians differ in their views on past events and, in particular, on the role of individuals in past events.

The study of history is an ongoing debate about events in the past. Although factual evidence is the essential ingredient of history, it is the *interpretation* of factual evidence that forms the basis for historical debate. The study of how and why historians differ in their various interpretations is termed 'historiography'.

Historical debate can occur for a wide variety of reasons.

Insufficient evidence

In some cases there is insufficient evidence to provide a definitive conclusion. In attempting to 'fill the gaps' where factual evidence is unavailable, historians use their professional judgement to make 'informed comments' about the past.

New evidence

As new evidence comes to light, an historian today may have more information on which to base judgements than historians in the past. For instance, major sources of information about 20th-century United States history are the presidential libraries of past presidents. Only when this information becomes available, can historians develop a more objective view of the past. This was the case with Robert Dallek's *Flawed Giant: Lyndon Johnson and His Times, 1961–1973* (1998).

A 'philosophy' of history?

Many historians have a specific view of history that will affect the way they make their historical judgements. For instance, Marxist historians – who take their view from the writings of Karl Marx, the founder of modern socialism – believe that society has always been made up of competing economic and social classes. They also place considerable importance on economic reasons behind human decision-making. Therefore, a Marxist historian looking at an historical issue may take a completely different viewpoint to a non-Marxist historian.

The role of the individual

Some historians have seen past history as being largely moulded by the acts of specific individuals. Presidents, such as Abraham Lincoln during the US Civil War or John F. Kennedy or Lyndon B. Johnson, can be picked out as having helped change US history. Other historians have tended to play down the role of individuals; instead, they highlight the importance of more general social, economic and political change. Rather than seeing Martin Luther King as the African-American leader who transformed the civil rights movement, these historians tend to see him as a representative of the educated African-American middle class in their attempt to gain full civil and political equality in the 1960s.

Placing different emphases on the same historical evidence

Even if historians do not possess different philosophies of history or place different emphasis on the role of the individual, it is still possible for them to disagree in one very important way. This is that they may place different emphases on aspects of the same factual evidence. As a result, History should be seen as a subject that encourages debate about the past, based on historical evidence.

Historians will always differ

Historical debate is, in its nature, continuous. What today may be an accepted view about a past event may well change in the future, as the debate continues.

Timeline: the lives of JFK & LBJ

JFK

LBJ

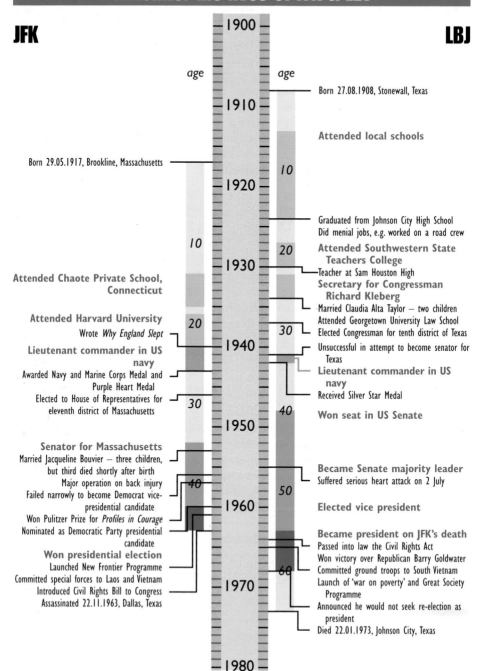

age — 1900

1910

age

Born 27.08.1908, Stonewall, Texas

Attended local schools

Born 29.05.1917, Brookline, Massachusetts

10

1920

10

Graduated from Johnson City High School
Did menial jobs, e.g. worked on a road crew

10

20

Attended Southwestern State
Teachers College

1930

Teacher at Sam Houston High

Attended Chaote Private School,
Connecticut

Secretary for Congressman
Richard Kleberg

Married Claudia Alta Taylor – two children

Attended Harvard University
Wrote *Why England Slept*

20

30

Attended Georgetown University Law School
Elected Congressman for tenth district of Texas

1940

Lieutenant commander in US
navy

Unsuccessful in attempt to become senator for
Texas

Awarded Navy and Marine Corps Medal and
Purple Heart Medal

Lieutenant commander in US
navy

Elected to House of Representatives for
eleventh district of Massachusetts

30

Received Silver Star Medal

40

1950

Won seat in US Senate

Senator for Massachusetts
Married Jacqueline Bouvier – three children,
but third died shortly after birth

Became Senate majority leader
Suffered serious heart attack on 2 July

Major operation on back injury
Failed narrowly to become Democrat vice-
presidential candidate

40

50

1960

Elected vice president

Won Pulitzer Prize for *Profiles in Courage*
Nominated as Democratic Party presidential
candidate

Became president on JFK's death
Passed into law the Civil Rights Act
Won victory over Republican Barry Goldwater

Won presidential election
Launched New Frontier Programme
Committed special forces to Laos and Vietnam
Introduced Civil Rights Bill to Congress
Assassinated 22.11.1963, Dallas, Texas

60

Committed ground troops to South Vietnam
Launch of 'war on poverty' and Great Society
Programme

1970

Announced he would not seek re-election as
president

Died 22.01.1973, Johnson City, Texas

1980

Vice President Lyndon B. Johnson with President John F. Kennedy.

JFK & LBJ: a brief joint biography

How did JFK and LBJ make history?

THE 1960s were a tumultuous time in American history. The USA faced a major crisis over civil rights for African-Americans. It also faced considerable social change as the young-adult generation developed new forms of music, fashion and behaviour. The 1960s were a decade of social revolution. The country was also bitterly divided over US involvement in the Vietnam War. America faced a decade of crisis that had not been seen since the US Civil War of 1861–5.

John Fitzgerald Kennedy and Lyndon Baines Johnson dominated the politics of the 1960s. At 43 years old, John F. Kennedy was the youngest president ever elected. He was the symbol of the new changes many Americans wanted to see. In his short presidency, from 1961 to 1963, he attempted to bring social reform and aided the cause for African-American civil rights. Perhaps most controversially, he involved the USA in the military defence of South Vietnam.

In many ways LBJ's presidency was a continuation of JFK's. Where JFK attempted social reform, LBJ became the most **reformist** president since the **New Deal of the 1930s**. He also was able to do more for African-American rights than any president had done since the US Civil War.

LBJ's most controversial act was the commitment of US ground troops to South Vietnam. By 1968, over 565 000 US troops were engaged in a vicious **guerrilla war**. So great was the financial cost of the war that it gravely damaged LBJ's social reform programme. More seriously, opposition to the war became so great within the USA that, in March 1968, LBJ decided not to seek re-election as president.

The period between 1961 and 1969 was one of great hope and expectation of change. It was also a period of political and social turmoil. The USA of today is still affected by the memory and experience of the Kennedy-Johnson years.

Upbringing, education and marriage

JFK and LBJ came from very different social backgrounds. Born in Brookline, Massachusetts, on 29 May 1917, John Fitzgerald Kennedy was the second son of Rose Fitzgerald and Joseph P. Kennedy (1888–1969). In total, Joseph Kennedy had nine children: four boys

Reformist: promoting political and social changes for the better.

New Deal of the 1930s: new relief policies put in place by President Franklin Delano Roosevelt (1933–45) to overcome the Great Depression.

Guerrilla war: war where one side is much more superior in numbers and equipment than the other side. In order to defeat the superior side, hit and run attacks are used by the weaker side to wear down the superior side's resolve to fight.

Robert Francis Kennedy (1925–68) Younger brother of John F. Kennedy, Robert F. Kennedy, managed JFK's successful campaign for US senator for Massachusetts in 1952. He also worked for the House Committee on Un-American Activities when Senator Joseph McCarthy was in charge. Following his brother's victory in the presidential campaign of 1960, Robert F. Kennedy was appointed attorney general in 1961. He played a key role in many foreign policies and was the administration's most important member, after his brother, in dealing with civil rights. He was elected senator for New York in 1964 and set up programmes to help the poor, the young and racial minorities. As senator, he began to criticise US involvement in the Vietnam War. On 18 March 1968, he announced his candidacy for president. He looked like winning nomination when he was assassinated in Los Angeles, California, on 5 June 1968, by Palestinian Sirhan Sirhan .

Addison's disease: a condition caused by a deficiency of the hormones made in the adrenal cortex. Symptoms include fatigue, muscle weakness, low blood pressure and brown discoloration of the skin.

and five girls. His ancestors were Irish farmers who emigrated to Boston, Massachusetts. As Irish-American Roman Catholics, the Kennedys faced discrimination from the rich Protestants who controlled Massachusetts' political and economic life. Nevertheless, Joseph Kennedy became a multimillionaire. He owned banks and even a Hollywood film studio. He also had personal dealings with the leaders of the Democratic Party. Through his political influence and money, he was determined that his sons would have successful political careers.

JFK was sent to the finest schools. From 1931 to 1935 he attended Chaote Academy, a private school, in Connecticut. From 1936 to 1940, he attended Harvard University – the most prestigious university in the USA. In 1938, his father was made US Ambassador to Britain and JFK made a summer visit to London and countries in Europe. In 1940 he wrote *Why England Slept* – a book that criticised Britain's policy towards Hitler. It became a bestseller.

Lyndon Baines Johnson, in complete contrast, was born into a poor family, on 27 August 1908, in the hill country of central Texas. He was the first of five children born to Sam Ealy Johnson and Rebekah Baines. While JFK's main influence during his youth was his father, it was LBJ's mother who was his dominant parental influence. She gave LBJ the belief that education was important for career advancement. As the eldest child, LBJ attended local state schools. He attended a teacher training college at San Marcos, Texas and, in 1930, he took a job as a school teacher at Sam Houston High School, San Marcos.

Both JFK and LBJ had political family backgrounds. JFK's grandfather, Patrick Kennedy, had been a state senator in Massachusetts. On his mother's side, his grandfather, John F. (Honey Fitz) Fitzgerald, had been a congressman and mayor of Boston. LBJ's grandfather and father had both been elected to the Texas State Legislature and, as a youth, LBJ had helped his father in election campaigns.

JFK always gave the impression of being fit and athletic. However, throughout his adult life, he was badly affected by back pain. In 1953, he underwent two life-threatening operations to deal with this problem. He also suffered from **Addison's disease**. His younger brother, **Robert Francis Kennedy**, stated that there wasn't a day when JFK was president that he didn't suffer pain.

LBJ also gave the impression of being very fit. He was a Texan rancher most of his adult life. However, in 1955, he suffered a serious heart attack. He was concerned about his health for the rest of his life.

In 1953, JFK married Jacqueline Bouvier, in the upper-class society wedding of the year. They went on to have three children: John, Caroline and Patrick. Patrick, however, died within a few hours of birth in August 1963.

LBJ met Claudia Taylor in the autumn of 1934. He proposed marriage on their first date. They married in November 1934 and went on to have two daughters: Lynda Bird and Lucy Baines.

Entering the political world

LBJ was first to enter national politics. In 1932, he became an assistant, in Washington DC, to Texan Congressman Richard Kleberg. In 1935, he became the Texas director of the **National Youth Administration (NYA).** Finally, in 1937, at the age of only 28, he was elected to the House of Representatives for the tenth district of Texas. Unfortunately, in 1941, LBJ had his first major political setback. He tried to become senator for Texas. He was narrowly defeated by Governor W. Lee O'Daniel in a close-fought contest that was noted for electoral fraud. Finally, in 1948, LBJ entered the Senate in another close-run contest in which electoral fraud was also a feature.

National Youth Administration (NYA): a programme, designed by Franklin Roosevelt, to provide vocational training for unemployed youths and part-time employment for needy students.

Both JFK and LBJ served in the Second World War. LBJ became a lieutenant commander in the navy. In 1942, he received the Silver Star from General Douglas MacArthur for gallantry in the South Pacific. JFK was a war hero. In 1943, the PT (motor torpedo) boat, which he commanded, was sunk by a Japanese destroyer. His heroism in saving his crew earned him the Navy and Marine Corps Medal. In 1944, JFK's elder brother, Joseph P. Kennedy Jr., was killed in action. From that date, JFK's father was determined to make his son a successful politician.

In 1946, JFK was elected for the eleventh Congressional district of Massachusetts. He was 29 years old; just one year older than LBJ had been when he entered Congress in 1937. In 1952, JFK became senator for Massachusetts.

During the 1950s, JFK was seen as a junior to LBJ in the Senate. In 1951, LBJ became Democrat Party whip and, in 1955, he became Senate majority leader. Through his influence and powers of persuasion, LBJ became the most powerful Senate leader in the 20th century. He often referred to JFK as 'the boy.'

Nevertheless, in 1956, JFK almost became Democratic vice-presidential candidate. His rise to the top of national politics was aided, in January 1956, when he won the prestigious Pulitzer Prize for his study of US history in his book *Profiles in Courage*. In 1960,

Understanding JFK and LBJ

- JFK was the first Roman Catholic to be elected as president.

- LBJ was the first Southerner to be elected as president since before the US Civil War of 1861–5.

- JFK was a charming, handsome, well-educated man from the upper class of US society in New England.

- LBJ came from a poor background, had rather crude manners and came from Texas.

- Both JFK and LBJ were Liberal Democrats who wanted to continue the New Deal social reforms of Franklin D. Roosevelt. JFK's programme, the New Frontier, and LBJ's programme, the Great Society, aimed to help the poor and needy.

- JFK was an effective public speaker and writer having won the Pulitzer Prize. However, he lacked the powers of political persuasion that were needed to be successful in working with Congress.

- LBJ was a poor public speaker, but he had considerable persuasive powers and worked very successfully with Congress.

- Both presidents were reluctant to champion the cause of African-American Civil Rights, yet they played a key role in bringing civil equality for all Americans.

- Both presidents were fervent anti-communists. They both believed in a worldwide communist conspiracy and the '**domino theory**' in South East Asia.

- JFK had a keen interest in American history, culture and achievement. While both men were eager to promote the arts and American achievement, JFK's enthusiasm was the greater of the two men. He regularly invited artists, writers, scientists, poets, musicians and actors to the White House.

'Domino theory': a belief held by presidents Eisenhower, Kennedy and Johnson. It stated that if only one country fell to communism in South East Asia it would lead to all South East Asian countries eventually falling to communism. Eisenhower used the analogy of a set of falling dominoes.

'JFK had an intellectual concern for the poor. LBJ felt the issue of poverty in his gut.'
Historian William H. Chafe

he beat LBJ to the position of Democratic presidential candidate. This was due, in part, to his father's money and influence and to his own effective campaigning.

In 1960, in one of the closest presidential elections, JFK narrowly defeated Richard Nixon. An important reason for JFK's victory was his decision to choose LBJ as his vice-presidential running mate. In the election, LBJ helped win Texas for JFK.

The Kennedy presidency

JFK's presidency was cut short on 22 November 1963 when he was assassinated in Dallas, Texas. As a young, martyred president, JFK has been seen as a potentially great president. In foreign affairs, he had a great triumph in the Cuban Missile Crisis of October 1962 when Soviet nuclear missiles were withdrawn from Cuba. However, he also had many failures. In April 1961, a **Central Intelligence Agency (CIA)** plot to invade Cuba failed badly. It was the Bay of Pigs Fiasco. In domestic affairs, he faced a coalition of conservative Democrats and Republicans who helped prevent many of his proposed reforms becoming law. It is difficult to know whether or not JFK would have succeeded in foreign and domestic affairs if he had lived. On 22 November 1963, LBJ became president. He had the task of fulfilling many of JFK's promises.

Central Intelligence Agency (CIA): branch of US Government that works to defend US interests. In the 1960s, it organised mercenary troops to fight communists, and engaged in surveillance and assassination of political opponents.

Lyndon B. Johnson sworn into office upon assassination of President Kennedy.

LBJ takes over

LBJ delivered where JFK had promised. From 1963 to 1966, LBJ was able to pass a whirlwind of social reform through Congress. His Great Society Programme was a continuation of JFK's New Frontier Programme, but it also went much further in an attempt to eradicate poverty from the USA. Almost all aspects of US life were affected by LBJ's reforms: civil rights, health, education, the environment, inner-city regeneration.

In foreign affairs, LBJ had to deal with the legacy of JFK's military support of the South Vietnamese Government. When JFK was assassinated, the US had 16 000 military advisers in South Vietnam. From 1965, LBJ greatly increased US involvement. South Vietnam's war against the communists became America's war. Over 565 000 US troops, at the cost of $60 million a day, meant that Vietnam, by 1968, was the dominant issue in US politics. Vietnam helped undermine the Great Society. It also destroyed LBJ's presidency. By the spring of 1968, the USA was bitterly divided over US involvement in the war. On 31 March LBJ announced, on national television, that he would stand down as president in January 1969.

Johnson's presidency began so well. It ended in political humiliation.

The legacy

Today, JFK is still seen as the martyred president. His body lies in Arlington National Cemetery, in Washington DC. An eternal flame marks his grave, which is visited by tens of thousands of people each year. Historians and political commentators have argued for decades about what JFK might have achieved if he had not been assassinated.

LBJ left national politics in January 1969. He returned to his ranch near Johnson City where he died in January 1973. He is buried there. Only a few hundred visitors come each year to visit the grave of someone described as a 'flawed giant'.

Despite their failures and flaws, both Kennedy and Johnson shall be remembered for facing great crises and for their great influence during a decade of momentous change in US history.

1

Who was more effective in domestic reform: JFK or LBJ?

How successful was Kennedy's New Frontier Programme?

How 'great' was Johnson's Great Society Programme?

Framework of events

1961	JFK sworn in as thirty-fifth president of United States
	Launch of New Frontier Programme
	Council of Economic Advisers created
	Minimum Wage Act
	School Assistance Bill fails to pass Congress
	Health care for elderly fails to pass Congress
	Housing Act
	Area Redevelopment Act
1962	Trade Expansion Act
	Manpower Development and Training Act
1963	Equal Pay Act
	Clean Air Act
	JFK discusses 'war on poverty' with advisers
	Assassination of JFK
	Lyndon Johnson becomes thirty-sixth president of United States
1964	Tax Reduction Act
	Economic Opportunity Act
	National Wilderness Preservation Act
1965	Elementary and Secondary Education Act
	Higher Education Act
	Medicare Act
	Medicaid Act
	Omnibus Housing Act
	Appalachian Regional Development Act
	National Endowment of the Arts Act
	Water Quality Control Act

1966	Demonstration Cities and Metropolitan Development Act
	Urban Mass Transportation Act
	Highways Beautification Act
1967	Air Quality Act
1968	Wild and Scenic Rivers Act
	Housing Act
	Occupational Health and Safety Act

BETWEEN 1961 and 1969, the USA was led by two administrations that put domestic reform at the centre of their agenda. From 1961 to 1963, John F. Kennedy proclaimed the New Frontier Programme. The title of this plan conjured up images of America's past and the 'pioneer spirit'. JFK saw a 'new frontier' of challenges. Kennedy stated, in a speech while campaigning for president on 29 October 1960, at **Valley Forge**, Pennsylvania:

Valley Forge: the place, during the American War of Independence where George Washington saved the American army from destruction.

> 'Twenty-four years ago, Franklin Roosevelt told the Nation "I, for one, do not believe that the era of the pioneer is at an end; I only believe that the area for pioneering has changed." The new frontiers of which I speak call out for pioneers from every walk of life.'

Kennedy planned a programme of major domestic reform that included education, health care and helping the poor.

When Kennedy was assassinated, his vice president, Lyndon B. Johnson, entered the White House. From 1963 to 1969, Johnson engaged in a great domestic reform programme, known as the Great Society, with a specific emphasis on a 'war on poverty'.

How successful was Kennedy's New Frontier Programme?

What was the New Frontier Programme?

When JFK was sworn in as president on 20 January 1961, he set out the broad goals of his New Frontier Programme. He stated:

> '... we stand today on a new frontier, a frontier that will demand of us all qualities of courage and conviction. For we are moving into the most challenging, the most dynamic, revolutionary period of our existence – the 1960s. The next 10 years will be

The American Government: a brief introduction

- The United States is a federal state. This means political power is split between a central, or federal, government and 50 state governments. State governments have direct responsibility for social security, education and law and order within their own state. During the 20th century, the **Federal Government** became involved in these areas of policy.

- The USA chooses a president every four years. The president is elected in early November and takes up office on 20 January.

- The president chooses the government. The leading members of the government form the Cabinet. The president also has many personal advisers. These usually work for the Executive Office of the president.

- Unlike Britain, no government member can be a member of the national parliament called Congress. This idea is called the separation of powers. In practice, it means the president can govern only with the cooperation of Congress.

- The Congress comprises the Senate (100 members) and the House of Representatives (435 members).

- The House of Representatives and one third of the Senate are elected every two years. Each state elects two senators. The House comprises of 435 congressmen who are chosen on a basis of state population. Populous states, such as California and New York, have many more congressmen than states such as Montana or Rhode Island.

- The president can propose legislation but Congress passes these proposals into law.

- A president can veto Congressional legislation but, if two thirds of Congress agrees, the presidential veto can be overridden.

- Even if the president and Congress agree, the US Supreme Court can declare a law or action by the president unconstitutional.

Federal Government: the national government.

years of incredible growth and change – years of unprecedented tasks for the next president of the United States.'

The whole tone of JFK's speech suggested major challenges and changes. The 1950s had been a decade where the Republican President Dwight Eisenhower wanted to preserve rather than change American society. Both JFK and LBJ wanted to deal directly with problems at home and wanted to ensure that the USA confronted communism abroad. They wanted the USA to be seen as the leader of the Free World against the USSR and Communist China and so they could not afford social divisions at home.

On the surface, it might seem that the USA required little social change. The 1960 census showed that the USA's 180 million people were the most affluent in the world. Per capita income had risen from $1501 in 1950 to $2219 in 1960. Even though **inflation** had reduced, a 50% growth in personal wealth was still very impressive. However, when Kennedy took office, the US economy was in **recession**. There was 6.5% unemployment and inflation at 3.5%. In addition, there were groups and areas in the country that had not benefited from the affluence of the 1950s. **Appalachia** was one area that suffered economic hardship. Also, the elderly and those on low incomes had missed out on '**the American dream**'. In preparation for office, JFK had set up a number of task forces to investigate different areas of policy. One group, under Senator Paul Douglas of Illinois, reported to Kennedy on depressed areas. Such reports played an important role in shaping JFK's domestic policy.

Some historians believe that the domestic programme was a reaction to the challenges of the Cold War. According to historian James N. Giglio, in *The Presidency of John F. Kennedy* (1991), 'The New Frontier embraced the past as much as it did the present.' In this sense, Kennedy was completing the work begun by the previous Democrat presidents, Frank D. Roosevelt (1933–45) and Harry S. Truman (1945–53). Under Roosevelt, the USA had been transformed by the social policies of the New Deal. These policies were continued with Truman's Fair Deal. After the brief interlude of Eisenhower's administration (1953–61), social reform was back at the centre of the domestic programme. Policies such as federal support for health care for the elderly had been a policy originally put forward by President Truman.

Inflation: an increase in the general level of prices.

Recession: a period of economic stagnation when unemployment rises as production falls.

Appalachia: mountainous area of eastern USA, which covers parts of West Virginia, Virginia, North Carolina, Kentucky, Tennessee and Georgia.

'The American dream': the belief that the USA has no discrimination against a person's background, either in wealth or race; the belief that if a person is intelligent enough and works hard they can 'reach the top'.

Opposition to the New Frontier

In *The Unfinished Journey: America Since World War II* (1999), historian William H. Chafe provides a brief assessment of Kennedy's period as president. He believes:

> There was something larger than life about the man, his presidency, his death, and his impact on the American people.

Many contemporaries believed that the youthful Kennedy, his dynamism and style, represented the new generation. They believed that his tragic death cut short a presidential career of great promise. Such views are supported in the works of several of Kennedy's close associates. These works include *Kennedy* (1965), by his presidential counsel, Theodore Sorensen, and *A Thousand Days: John F. Kennedy in the White House* (1965), by Arthur M. Schlesinger. However, some people consider the reality of JFK's period as president to be very different. BBC journalist Henry Fairlie claims, in *The Kennedy Promise* (1973), that JFK's New Frontier was a complete failure.

In many ways, Henry Fairlie's assessment is nearer the truth. American political scientist, Richard E. Neustadt, stated, 'Presidential power is the power to persuade.' For all his personal charm, JFK found it very difficult to persuade Congress to pass his New Frontier Programme.

First, Kennedy lacked a strong political mandate. He had won the presidency by the slimmest of margins. He won by 118 574 votes out of 68 million cast. His Electoral College victory of 303 to Nixon's 219 was due to paper-thin victories in a number of states. JFK then had to deal with many senators and congressmen who had won by large majorities and had years, if not decades, of political experience at national level.

Second, with Lyndon Johnson as his vice president, JFK had lost a Senate majority leader who could have helped him with the passage of his New Frontier Programme. Instead, JFK relied heavily on a close aide, Larry O'Brien, to persuade Congress. O'Brien lacked LBJ's ability and contacts.

Finally, and perhaps most significantly, Kennedy faced a **conservative coalition** in Congress. Such a coalition had been in existence since FDR tried to reform the US Supreme Court in 1937.

To make matters worse, key post holders within Congress were hostile to the New Frontier. Senate minority leader, Republican Charles Halleck of Indiana felt that JFK had 'stolen' the 1960s election. He remained a fierce opponent. Congress was also dominated by committee chairmen who had the power to delay and even 'kill off' presidential proposals for legislation. One of the most powerful positions was chairman of the House Rules Committee. He

Conservative coalition: informal group of senators and congressmen. The group comprised of Republicans and Southern white Democrats. They opposed social reform and improvements in African-American civil rights.

**Wilbur Daigh Mills
(1909–92)**
Mills was a congressman from Arkansas who had received a law degree from Harvard University. He was a member of the House of Representatives from 1939 to 1977 and chairman of the House Ways and Means Committee during Kennedy's and Johnson's presidencies. In 1972, he ran for Democrat nomination for president, but was unsuccessful. His career effectively came to an end in 1974 when he was caught drink-driving in Washington DC with a stripper called Fenne Foxe, known as the Argentinean Firecracker.

US Constitution: the document that contains the rules and regulations that govern political activity in the USA. It was drawn up in 1787 and finally agreed by all original 13 states in 1791. It has been amended 26 times since 1787. The first 10 amendments were in 1791.

had the power to assign Bills (proposals for legislation) to specific subject committees such as agriculture, finance, foreign affairs, and so on. In 1961, the chairman was archconservative South Democrat Howard W. Smith of Virginia. He bragged that he would turn JFK into a 'do nothing' president. Fortunately, with the assistance of the speaker of the House of Representatives, Sam Rayburn, JFK was able to oust Smith from his post on 31 January 1961. By enlarging the membership of the House Rules Committee, JFK won the vote 217 to 212. Ominously, 22 Republicans and 64 Southern Democrats voted against JFK.

Reform in five areas

In January 1961, Kennedy wanted to pass legislation in five key areas: federal assistance to schools, medical care for the elderly, housing reform, aid to depressed areas and an increase in the minimum wage.

In education reform, the New Frontier could be judged a failure. In February 1961, JFK submitted a School Assistance Bill to Congress. He asked for $2.3 billion over three years to help construct new schools and to increase teachers' salaries. As a Roman Catholic, he was sensitive to the issue of Catholic Church schools. However, the first amendment of the **US Constitution** stated that the Church was separate from the state and so the Assistance Bill did not cover Catholic schools. The USA's Catholic bishops therefore opposed the Bill and the USA's first Roman Catholic president! The Bill passed the Senate but was defeated in the House.

Health care for the elderly fared no better. JFK wanted to increase social security taxes by 0.25%. The House Ways and Means Committee effectively 'killed off' the proposal. Its chairman, **Wilbur Daigh Mills**, was a long-time opponent of the health care part of social security.

Fortunately for Kennedy, he did get an increase in the minimum wage. He proposed an increase to $1.25 per hour. Although Congress passed this, important groups of workers were excluded from the minimum wage. South Democrat opposition, led by Carl Vinson of Georgia, made sure that 150 000 laundry workers were excluded. The majority of laundry workers were female African-Americans. In total, 350 000 poorly paid workers were excluded from the Minimum Wage Act.

The Area Redevelopment Act of 1961 was also passed. This

provided $394 million over four years to aid areas such as Appalachia. Although around 26 000 new jobs were created under the Act, an attempt to give more money ($455 million), in 1963, failed to pass Congress. The Manpower Development and Training Act of 1962 had greater impact. This provided job training for the poorly educated across 40 states that had applied for funding.

President Kennedy speaking at the opening ceremony of the USA's largest cooperative housing development, Manhattan, 1962.

The Housing Act of 1961 was of greater success. Kennedy got Congress to give $4.8 billion to fund housing projects for the poor. However, Congress acted mainly to help the US out of the 1960/1 economic recession rather than to show long-term sympathy for the poor.

Kennedy's legislative record had mixed success by the time of his assassination. Historian James Giglio, in *The Presidency of John F. Kennedy* (1991), claims that JFK's record was impressive. He cites, as evidence, the fact that in 1961, 33 out of 53 major recommendations to Congress became law. In 1962, the figure was 41 out of 54 and in 1963, 35 out of 58. Giglio suggests that this is a good record compared to other presidents since 1935. However, out of JFK's five 'must' Bills of 1961, the three that passed into law were amended in a radical way by a conservative-dominated Congress. In *Decade of Disillusionment: The Kennedy-Johnson Years* (1975), historian Jim F. Heath declares:

Landmark Study | **The book that changed people's views**

J.F. Heath, *Decade of Disillusionment: The Kennedy-Johnson Years* (Indiana University Press, 1975)

This was the first major critical study of the Kennedy-Johnson years in domestic policy as one unified period of history. It followed several very favourable studies of Kennedy written by close associates such as Theodore Sorensen and Arthur Schlesinger. It also followed several critical studies of Johnson such as *Lyndon Johnson and the Exercise of Power* (1966), by Rowland Evans and Robert Novak.

Heath used the Kennedy and Johnson libraries extensively for research. In particular, he used oral histories and transcripts of interviews. Heath took the view that the Kennedy-Johnson years were a period of a missed opportunity in the midst of a major social revolution within the United States. Both presidents had great dreams and hopes for the USA but as Heath states:

The two presidents believed that they could shape the destinies of the United States by a combination of will and pragmatic knowledge. Their dreams and hopes were shattered by intractable forces beyond their control, though often of their own making.

Heath stresses the strong element of continuity in the liberal views of the two presidents. Although he regards Johnson as a radical reformer, he believes Johnson merely finishes the work of FDR's New Deal rather than developed completely new ideas.

One suspects that considering what he concretely achieved – not proposed or hoped to achieve – Kennedy would rank his own domestic record as disappointing. Although his programmes were designed to aid and advance the welfare state, Kennedy was decidedly not even a committed social reformer. Kennedy moved cautiously in the comfortable ruts worn by Roosevelt, Truman and even Eisenhower. (See **Landmark Study** above.)

How 'great' was Johnson's Great Society Programme?

Did Johnson continue the New Frontier Programme when he became president?

Kennedy's presidency was cut short by an assassin's bullet on 22 November 1963. When Lyndon Johnson became president he made sure that he would gain popularity and acceptance by publicly linking himself with the martyred president. In a speech to the joint houses of Congress on 27 November 1963, Johnson made clear his immediate aim as president. He declared:

'All I have, I would have given gladly not to be standing here today … let us continue, let us here highly resolve that John Fitzgerald Kennedy did not live or die in vain … This is no time for delay. It is a time for action.'

Thus, Johnson used Kennedy's memory to push through important Acts of Kennedy's domestic programme.

The links with the New Frontier also went much deeper. Education, health care, and regional regeneration were all central planks of Johnson's own domestic programme. There was considerable overlap between the New Frontier and Johnson's own domestic programme, which he entitled the Great Society.

In broader context, both the New Frontier and the Great Society were part of a longer-term development in American domestic politics that went back at least as far as Franklin Roosevelt's New Deal of 1933–45. In that development the US Constitution required the Federal Government to 'promote the general welfare' of the US population. From 1933 to the 1960s, the Federal Government took a commanding role in dealing with the USA's domestic problems. The Kennedy-Johnson years saw the highest point of federal attempts to deal with domestic issues such as poverty.

Of the five 'must' bills at the start of Kennedy's presidency, Johnson continued work in a number of areas, most notably education, health care and aid to depressed areas.

Education

Kennedy tried and failed to pass the School Assistance Bill of 1961. When Johnson became president, education was given the top priority in domestic affairs. As a former schoolteacher, Johnson valued education as a way to help the poor to advance in the world. His own personal experience was central to this belief. When he signed the Elementary and Secondary Education Act into law on 11 April 1965, he stated:

> 'I believe deeply that no law I have signed or will ever sign means more to the future of America.'

1965 proved to be the high point in LBJ's educational policy. The Elementary and Secondary Education Act gave funds to school districts on the basis of the number of low-income families (those earning under $2000 per year). By 1968, 6.7 million poor children received assistance. This particularly benefited poor states such as Mississippi. The Act gave funds to improve library resources, textbooks and other school resources and it also aimed to encourage student participation in subjects such as art and music. Finally, the Act gave funding to aid children with disabilities. Over 26 000 students benefited. This aspect was a direct continuation of Kennedy's more cautious plans to aid disadvantaged students. Through **Executive Orders**, JFK had increased school lunch and milk programmes for the poor. This enabled 700 000 children to

Executive Order: a rule or regulation issued by the president to help implement an aspect of the US Constitution or an Act of Congress.

enjoy a daily free school lunch and free fresh milk. Enrolments in elementary schools increased from 39 million in 1962 to 46 million in 1970.

In 1965, Johnson persuaded Congress to pass the Higher Education Act. This granted federal scholarships for undergraduate students. It also gave students loans to pay for university education. By 1968, grants amounted to $131 million with loans of $182 million. Johnson broadened the scope of **Eisenhower's National Defense Education Act of 1958** and these reforms meant that the college-graduate population increased from 17.3% in 1962 to 23.4% in 1976.

Eisenhower's National Defense Education Act of 1958: this Act was passed in direct response to the USSR's successful launching of the first satellite in space, called *Sputnik*, in 1957. Eisenhower believed the USA was falling behind the USSR in technological education so this Act aimed to promote scientific and technical education.

Health care

Like Kennedy before him, Johnson was keen on providing welfare help for the elderly in health care. Unfortunately for Kennedy, the chairman of the House Ways and Means Committee, Wilbur Mills, obstructed his plan. Johnson, on the other hand, was able to use his influence in Congress to get the Medicare Act passed in 1965. As in JFK's proposal, this Act provided free health care for the elderly paid out of social security taxes.

In 1965, Johnson took his health care reforms further. This provided free health care for certain groups of the poor and people with disabilities below the age of 65.

Aid to depressed areas

Kennedy had had some success in providing help to areas facing economic problems. Like most of his legislative record he had moved cautiously.

In 1963, JFK read a newspaper review of a study entitled *The Other America* (1962), by Michael Harrington. Harrington argued that although most Americans had a high standard of living, 40 to 50 million Americans lived in poverty. Kennedy was so impressed by Harrington's work that he asked his advisers to draw up a plan to deal with the issue of the poor underclass. Unfortunately, JFK's assassination cut short this plan. However, Johnson continued the policy. The big difference came in terms of scale and ambition. According to Paul K. Conkin in his biography of LBJ, *Big Daddy from the Pedernales* (1986):

> Johnson's goal was to perfect every institution, to solve all pressing problems, to eliminate glaring inequalities and injustices, to realise the dream of equality for all.

In his State of the Union address of 8 January 1964, Johnson made clear how ambitious he was on the issue:

> 'This administration today, here and now, declares unconditional war on poverty in America.'

What was Johnson's 'war on poverty'?

Johnson's 'war on poverty' was the central plank of the Great Society Programme. Johnson turned the issue that Kennedy had talked briefly about before his death into a personal crusade. At the University of Michigan, on 22 May 1964, Johnson talked openly for the first time about creating the Great Society. As historian Paul Conkin notes:

> Johnson talked about a perfect America. He seemed to want to solve all its problems and to do it all quickly.

The cornerstone of the 'war on poverty' was the Economic Opportunity Act of 1964. The Act created a new federal agency – the Office of Economic Opportunity (OEO). JFK's brother-in-law, Sargent Shriver, who had run Kennedy's **Peace Corps**, headed it. The OEO had the task of coordinating a large number of schemes. Based on the Peace Corps, VISTA (Volunteers in Service to America) gave middle-class young people opportunities to help the needy

Peace Corps: an organisation created by JFK, which enabled US citizens to volunteer to work abroad, helping in Third World countries.

Johnson proudly holding out the Economic Opportunity Act, which he signed into law on 20 August 1964.

within the USA. By 1968, 3000 middle-class people had volunteered. The Head Start Programme gave poor children classes before they went to school. Jobs Corps aimed to offer skills training to inner-city youths. These programmes did have some success. Head Start involved eight million children. Jobs Corps found jobs for 10 000 youths. Its effectiveness was due, in part, to the involvement of firms such as IBM, the computer company.

The most controversial part of the Economic Opportunity Act was the creation of Community Action Programmes (CAPs). In *State and Society in Twentieth-Century America* (1997), historian Robert Harrison notes:

> [The CAP] was only part of the whole anti-poverty package, but by its explosive political impact it coloured public reaction to the whole enterprise.

The aim was to encourage new attitudes among the poor by allowing them to play a part in a federal programme. In part, it aimed to empower Southern black people in determining policies that affected them. Unfortunately, many CAPs, particularly in northern cities, were dominated by militants who criticised the Johnson administration for not doing enough. Johnson received criticism from within his own Democrat Party. Mayor Richard Daley of Chicago stated that involving the poor in the CAP was like 'telling the fellow that cleans up [at the newspaper] to be the city editor'. Sociologist Daniel Patrick Moynihan went further by saying:

> The programme [CAP] was carried out in such a way as to produce a minimum of social change its sponsors desired and to bring about a maximum increase in the opposition to such change.

Perhaps the most innovative Act passed to aid inner cities was the Demonstration Cities and Metropolitan Development Act of 1966. According to historian Paul Conkin, in *Big Daddy from the Pedernales: Lyndon Baines Johnson* (1986):

> … the major stated goal of the Act was to improve the quality of urban life 'the most critical domestic problem' facing the USA. Its main weapon was to be comprehensive demonstrative projects in slum or blighted areas, designed to improve the welfare of people who already lived there.

The Federal Government offered local governments 80% grants to deal with issues such as crime prevention, health care, recreation and job creation. In 1966, Congress authorised spending of $412 million that rose to $512 million in 1967. However, like CAPs, it was difficult to evaluate the success of the Demonstration Cities and Metropolitan Development Act. Suffice to say that in 1968 Congress cut off funding for the projects.

Johnson was determined to continue to help inner cities and, in 1968, he proposed the most ambitious federal housing initiative in US history. He proposed the building of 26 million housing units over 10 years. The Housing Act of 1968 authorised a total of $1.7 million for the first three years. The Act led to the building of cheap, rather poorly built homes. Builders and developers reduced their involvement because of limits on profits. When Richard Nixon became president, in 1969, he removed many restrictions on developers and reduced federal funding following scandals about the quality of the housing produced.

Johnson's policies to aid the poor and develop the economies of depressed regions went beyond inner cities. The Appalachian Regional Development Act of 1965 allocated $1.1 billion to programmes aimed to raise the standard of living in the Appalachian mountain area. This was a direct continuation of reform begun by Kennedy. The Omnibus Housing Act of 1965 was also a clear continuation of Kennedy's reform. The Act provided the construction of 240 000 houses and $2.9 million for urban renewal. Johnson achieved where Kennedy had failed.

The future Republican president, Ronald Reagan, claimed that in the 'war on poverty', poverty won! The over-ambitious claims of Johnson to eradicate poverty and the lack of coordination of federal programmes brought a political reaction against direct federal involvement in welfare. From 1969, the Federal Government reduced its role in welfare.

In *Liberalism and Its Challengers: From FDR to Bush* (1992), historian Alonzo L. Hamby declares that LBJ 'in his striving for hyper-accomplishment he simply tried to do too much.' Mark I. Gelfand in 'The War on Poverty', in *The Johnson Years* (1981), claims:

> Conservatives are prone to stress the shortcomings, label whole effort a failure and demand a rollback of federal intervention. Radicals are likely to employ similar characterisations but call for greater federal control.

However, according to the US Census, the number of families in poverty dropped from 40 million in 1959, to 28 million in 1968 and to just over 25 million in 1970. Part of this change can be attributed to a thriving economy. Johnson's 'war on poverty' clearly had a considerable impact on the USA, although not quite to the extent that he had planned.

Environment and consumer protection

By the early 1960s, the US Government was becoming more aware of the environmental effects of an advanced industrial society. An important catalyst for change was the book *Silent Spring* (1962), by Rachel Carson, a former member of the Federal Fish and Wildlife Service. She highlighted the indiscriminate use of chemicals such as DDT and its effects on the food chain. Ultimately the Federal Government would ban DDT in 1972.

During Kennedy's administration, the first steps were made to improve the environment of cities and urban areas with the Clean Air Act of 1963. This limited the pollution emissions from cars and factories. JFK also extended the National Park Service by approving legislation that made Padre Island and Point Reyes National Seashores.

Johnson went much further in the Great Society. He created a new Federal Pollution Control Administration. In his environment legislation, he amended Kennedy's Clean Air Act to make it more effective and supplemented it with the Water Quality Control Act 1965, the Water Resources Planning Act 1965, the Clean Water Restoration Act 1966 and the Air Quality Act 1967. The combined effect of this legislation made Johnson the most effective defender of the environment in US history to that time. Also, like Kennedy, he made direct attempts to extend the National Park Service. The National Wilderness Preservation Act of 1964 added 54 new areas to the National Park Service.

Johnson also became involved in the area of consumer protection in a way not seen since Theodore Roosevelt's presidency of 1901–9. The Fair Packaging and Labelling Act 1966, the Automobile Safety Act 1966, the Meat Inspection Act 1967, the Poultry Inspection Act 1967, the Coal Mine Safety Act 1967 and, most important of all, the Occupational Health and Safety Act 1968 provided US consumers and workers with effective protection.

Why was Johnson more successful than Kennedy in domestic affairs?

In his assessment of the Great Society, historian Paul Conkin, in *Big Daddy from the Pedernales: Lyndon Baines Johnson* (1986), notes:

> Johnson loved it. His domestic triumphs alone sustained him during the darkest days of the Vietnam War. What president ever did so much for the American people?

Veteran US diplomat William Averell Harriman observed:

LBJ was great in domestic affairs. Harry Truman had programmes, but none got through. Kennedy had no technique. If it hadn't been for … Vietnam he'd [LBJ] have been the greatest president ever.

This is borne out by looking at Johnson's legislative record. Historian Vaughn Davis Bornet, in *The Presidency of Lyndon B. Johnson* (1983), states:

The percentages of Johnsonian legislative successes are awesome: 1964 – 58[%]; 1965 – 69[%]; 1966 – 56[%]; 1967 – 48[%] and 1968 – 56[%].

During the eighty-ninth Congress, 1965/6, Johnson passed the bulk of his Great Society Programme. In achieving this remarkable success, Johnson had the support of a Senate and House dominated by Liberal Democrats. This was a far cry from the conservative coalition that had faced Kennedy. Nevertheless, Johnson himself recognised the debt he owed Kennedy and his legacy. In 1971, in retirement, Johnson wrote:

I never lost sight of the fact that I was trustee and custodian of the Kennedy administration.

However, whether Johnson realised it or not, his Great Society went far beyond anything that Kennedy had said or proposed. Johnson's administration of 1963–9 proved to be the most reforming administration in the 20th century.

Who was more effective in domestic reform: JFK or LBJ?

1. Read the following extract and answer the question.

   'Without the interest of Kennedy and, to a much greater degree Johnson, the "war on poverty" would never have been declared. It was Johnson's eagerness to seize on the sketchy pilot programmes that had been [made] under the Kennedy administration and convert them into a much larger, more comprehensive and more ambitious programme.'

   (R. Harrison, *State and Society in Twentieth-Century America* (Longman, 1997, p 297.)

   Using the information in the extract above, and from this section, explain whether Johnson's Great Society Programme was merely a continuation of Kennedy's New Frontier Programme.

2. What do you regard as the most successful domestic reform policy of the Kennedy-Johnson years? Explain your answer using information from this section.

2

Who did more for black civil rights: JFK or LBJ?

Was JFK forced by African-American activists to take action on civil rights?

Did Johnson merely fulfil Kennedy's legacy on civil rights?

Framework of events

1960	Feb	Lunch-counter protests begin, by SNCC members, in Greensboro, North Carolina
1961	May	'Freedom rides' begin by CORE members
1962	Oct	James Meredith is first African-American student to enrol at University of Mississippi
1963	Feb	Kennedy proposes Civil Rights Bill
	Apr	Demonstrations in Birmingham, Alabama, led by Martin Luther King
	Jun	JFK goes on national television to support a strong Civil Rights Bill following murder of NAACP leader, Medgar Evers
		Civil Rights Bill sent to Congress
	Aug	'March on Washington' and Martin Luther King's 'I have a dream' speech
1964	Jan	Poll tax amendment to US Constitution
	Jul	Congress passes the Civil Rights Act
1965	Mar	Martin Luther King leads Selma-to-Montgomery march against segregation
	Aug	Congress passes Voting Rights Act
		Black riots in Watts district of Los Angeles
1967	Jul	Black rioting in Newark, New Jersey and Detroit, Michigan
		Kerner Commission set up by Johnson to investigate causes of riots
	Oct	Thurgood Marshall becomes first African-American member of US Supreme Court
1968	Apr	Assassination of Martin Luther King followed by rioting in cities across America
		Congress passes Civil Rights Act

THE 1960s were a momentous decade in the history of African-American civil rights. Not since the Civil War (1861–5) and the Reconstruction era (1863–77), did African-American rights hold centre stage in US domestic politics. The decade was associated with a concerted attempt to end legal

Old South: the former States of the Confederacy (1861–5). It comprised of Mississippi, Louisiana, Arkansas, Texas, Alabama, Georgia, North and South Carolina, Virginia, Florida and Tennessee.

Pressure groups: political organisations that do not seek election to office but that attempt to influence or pressure politicians to follow a particular policy.

segregation and discrimination against African-Americans. This occurred predominantly in the **Old South**, which had comprised of the Confederacy during the Civil War. Action consisted of demonstrations and direct action by African-Americans. More noted among the **pressure groups** that fought for equal rights were the NAACP (National Association for the Advancement of Colored People), the CORE (Congress of Racial Equality) and the SNCC (Student Non-violent Coordinating Committee). These groups forced the USA to accept the moral dilemma that it was the leader of the free world against communism but denied a large proportion of its citizens full civil and political rights. Kennedy and Johnson had to confront this issue and played an integral part in gaining full civil and political rights for African-Americans.

African-Americans in 1961

In 1961, African-Americans numbered 18.8 million or 10.5% of the US population. Traditionally they had lived in the Old South. However, by 1960, following the 'great migration' of the 1920s–40s, African-Americans also comprised an important proportion of the population of the cities outside that area. In 1960, they comprised 53.9% of Washington DC, the capital. They also comprised 34.9% of Baltimore, Maryland, 28.9% of Detroit, Michigan and 22.9% of Chicago, Illinois. The African-Americans outside the Old South tended to live in inner-city ghettoes. In 1965, 43% of all African-American families were living below the poverty line, earning under $3000 per year.

Under the US Constitution, African-Americans should have had the same political and civil rights as all other Americans. The thirteenth, fourteenth and fifteenth amendments of the Constitution, passed between 1865 and 1870 gave them full rights. However, from 1877, state governments in the Old South had led the way in passing Jim Crow laws. These laws provided separate facilities for African-Americans in virtually everything from education, to housing and recreation. A landmark decision by the US Supreme Court in 1954 led the way towards ending this system. In Brown versus Board of Education of Topeka, the Court declared that having separate schools for black and white students was unconstitutional. However, by 1961, only very limited change had occurred in removing Jim Crow laws. African-Americans across most of the Old South were still second-class citizens.

Was JFK forced by African-American activists to take action on civil rights?

The Kennedy and Johnson record on civil rights before 1961

There is little evidence to show that either JFK or LBJ had a strong desire to support civil and political equality for African-Americans. According to journalist and family friend of the Kennedys', Arthur Krock, JFK 'never saw a Negro on social-level terms'. Kennedy came from Massachusetts, which possessed only a small African-American population. Johnson was similar. The main ethnic minority that Johnson had contact with, before starting his political career, were Hispanic Americans in San Marcos, Texas.

Both politicians had the ambition to rise to the top of the Democratic Party. To do so they needed the support of Southern white Democrats. Throughout the 1950s, Kennedy sought to avoid upsetting Southern Democrats – so much so that the NAACP regarded Senator Kennedy with suspicion.

In 1957, Kennedy went so far as to criticise President Eisenhower's dispatch of troops to protect the African-American students who wished to enrol at Central High School, in **Little Rock**. In the same year, JFK voted with Southern Democrats for the **pro-jury trial amendment** to the Civil Rights Bill. This greatly reduced the Act's effectiveness in defending African-American civil rights. Even when he won office in 1960, Kennedy informed black leaders that he did not plan to introduce any civil rights legislation in 1961.

Johnson also avoided conflict with the people who were his natural constituency. LBJ's great mentor in the Senate was Richard Russell of Georgia. He was a leading segregationist. Also, from 1955 to 1960, Johnson was Senate majority leader and to be successful he had to keep Southern Democrats on his side. Southern Democrats held the chairs of the most important Senate committees. Although two civil rights Acts were passed, in 1957 and 1960, when Johnson was Senate majority leader, he made sure that the legislation made little difference to white domination of Southern politics.

How did Kennedy defend civil rights during his presidency?

There is considerable evidence to suggest that Kennedy reacted to events rather than took a positive stand on African-American civil

Little Rock: in the autumn of 1957, nine black students attempted to enrol at Central High School, Little Rock, Arkansas. The governor of Arkansas, Orvil Faubus, attempted to prevent their enrolment and was supported by white segregationists. To allow the students the right of enrolment, President Eisenhower sent the 101st Airborne Division to Little Rock to force compliance with federal law, which forbade segregation in public schools.

Pro-jury trial amendment: white juries in the Old South could amend legislation against African-American voter registration.

Lunch-counter protest by African-American students at Woolworth's, Greensboro, 1960.

rights. During the presidential election year of 1960, civil rights became national news with lunch-counter protests by black students. Starting at the F.W. Woolworth department store in Greensboro, North Carolina, students of the SNCC began a sit-down protest to force Woolworth's to serve black as well as white customers. In February 1961, other black and white students adopted similar non-violent protests against segregation in inner-state bus travel. Students of CORE tested federal law by travelling through the Old South on 'Greyhound' interstate buses. When they reached Anniston, Alabama, white protesters firebombed their bus.

Confronted with an inflammatory situation, JFK relied on his brother, Attorney General Robert F. Kennedy, to deflate the situation. He sent federal marshals to aid the students. In *Sweet Land of Liberty?: The African-American Struggle for Civil Rights in the Twentieth Century* (1998), historian Robert Cook notes:

> The dispatch of US marshals revealed the extent to which the Kennedys had been embarrassed by media coverage of the 'freedom ride'.

The 'freedom rides' and Robert Kennedy's involvement are explained in some depth in episode 3 of the television series *The Eyes on the*

Landmark Study — The television series that changed people's views

R. Lavelle (Project director), *The Eyes on the Prize* (Public broadcasting system of USA, 1987 and 1990)

Blackside Inc, an African-American owned production company, over the course of 12 years, produced a 14-part history of African-American civil rights from 1954 to 1985. The first six-part series covers 1954 to 1965 and is entitled the 'Civil Rights Years, 1954–1965'. It was shown on US television between January and February 1987. The second eight-part continuation series covers 1965 to 1985 and is entitled 'America at the Crossroads, 1965–1985'. This was shown on US television in 1990.

The series uses archival footage and contemporary and retrospective interviews with people involved in the civil rights struggle, including Kennedy's and Johnson's aides. Not only is it an invaluable source for historians and educators but, when shown in 1987 and 1990, it reached an entire generation of Americans who had not experienced the civil rights struggle. Each one-hour episode was watched by 20 million viewers. The series won 23 major awards including two Emmys.

Episode 4: 'No Easy Walk, 1961–1963' covers James Meredith at Mississippi University, the riots in Birmingham, Alabama 1963 and the 'March on Washington'. Episode 6: 'Bridge to Freedom, 1965' deals with the events leading to the passage of the Voting Rights Act. Episode 7: 'The Time has Come, 1964–1966' details the height of Johnson's involvement in civil rights.

Prize (see **Landmark Study** above). Kennedy had almost daily telephone contact with the state authorities in Alabama. However, the Kennedys were reluctant to force the issue of desegregation. Arthur M. Schlesinger, in *Robert Kennedy and His Times* (1978), notes that by protecting the 'freedom riders' but not forcing desegregation, Robert F. Kennedy 'became almost as unpopular among civil rights workers as he was among segregationists'.

Schlesinger's critical view of the Kennedy stance on civil rights is borne out by other historians. In *The Civil Rights Movement: Struggle and Resistance* (1997), William T. Martin Riches notes:

> Although the election of JFK was largely due to the African-American vote, his appointment of his brother Robert as attorney general did not augur well for those involved in the civil rights movement.

Irving Bernstein, in *From Promises Kept: John F. Kennedy's New Frontier* (1991), notes:

> … [JFK] had not known many black people, knew little about segregation, and had not considered the federal role in promoting desegregation.

Nevertheless, pressure was placed on the Interstate Commerce Commission, by the administration, to ban segregation in interstate bus terminals. This enforced the 1958 US Supreme Court decision of Boynton versus Virginia, which had declared such practices unconstitutional.

Martin Luther King (1929–68)
King was born in Atlanta, Georgia. By the time he became a Baptist minister, in 1954, he was a civil rights campaigner for African-Americans and a member of the National Association for the Advancement of Colored people.

He first came to national attention as leader of the Montgomery bus boycott of 1955/6. In 1957, he was elected president of the Southern Christian Leadership Conference – an organisation formed to provide new leadership for the civil rights movement. King was a brilliant speaker and between 1957

and his death in 1968 he spoke over 2500 times about injustice, protest and action. In 1964, he was awarded the Nobel Peace Prize. On the evening of 4 April his life was brought to an untimely end when he was assassinated by a lone, white gunman in Memphis, Tennessee.

Following the 'freedom rides', John Kennedy wanted to avoid any other confrontation in the South that would force him to act. JFK had major problems with the conservative coalition in Congress. The Southern white Democrat committee chairman was stalling much of his New Frontier domestic programme. Kennedy feared another Little Rock episode.

Unfortunately, in 1962, Kennedy was faced with this type of problem when African-American James Meredith applied to take a law degree at the all-white University of Mississippi. The Democrat Party within Mississippi was split between moderates and extremists. Governor Ross Barnett, who was completely against desegregation, led the latter. Attempts at peaceful enrolment came to nothing. In the television series *The Eyes on the Prize*, Kennedy is shown telephoning Ross Barnett as part of a plan to find a peaceful solution to the problem. In the end, Robert F. Kennedy decided to send 170 US federal marshals and Deputy Attorney General Nicholas Katzenbach to Mississippi University. An all-night riot on 1 October 1962 between white segregationists and the US marshals left two dead and over 100 people injured. The Kennedys sent in 30 000 troops to restore order.

JFK was equally reactive in his attitude to the civil rights movement when **Martin Luther King** organised demonstrations in Birmingham, Alabama in April–May 1963. The televised scenes of police dogs and water hoses to disperse demonstrators, who included children and pregnant women, shocked the people. It also acted as a major landmark in the education of the Kennedy brothers in the extent of discrimination against African-Americans in the Old South. In *To Redeem the Soul of America: The Southern Christian Leadership Conference and Martin Luther King, Jr.* (1987), historian Adam Fairclough states:

The success of Birmingham should not be judged according to its impact on Congress. The evidence strongly suggests that the SCLC's demonstrations played a decisive role in persuading the Kennedy administration to introduce legislation.

As shown in *The Eyes on the Prize*, JFK gave a nationally televised speech on 11 June 1963 in support of further civil rights for African-Americans.

However, historian James N. Giglio, in *The Presidency of John F. Kennedy* (1991), believes JFK began to change his view earlier. He believes JFK's proactive view on civil rights dates from late 1962, which was:

> ... a time of frustration for the administration over growing Southern violence, the slowness of civil rights advances, and criticism from virtually all civil rights groups.

He believes 'Kennedy recognised the discontent and perceived need for action'.

Action took the form of a very modest Civil Rights Bill sent to Congress in February 1963. This aimed to improve African-American voting rights and to assist the desegregation of public schools. However, the chance of even this surviving the opposition

Attorney General Robert Kennedy talks to civil rights marchers in Washington in 1963.

of the conservative coalition looked slender. Nevertheless, JFK supported the '**March on Washington**', in August 1963, which brought the whole civil rights issue to the seat of government.

Kennedy was fortunate that his presidency coincided with two constitutional amendments that benefited African-Americans. On 29 March 1961 the United States ratified the twenty-third amendment, which had been proposed in June 1960. This gave the citizens of the district of Columbia the right to vote in presidential elections. Washington DC had a black majority by late 1961. On 27 March 1962, the twenty-fourth amendment was submitted to Congress. When ratification was completed, on 23 January 1964, poor black and white people were no longer prevented from voting 'by reason of failure to pay any poll tax or other tax'.

Politics is the art of the possible. Given the political conditions of Kennedy's presidency, it could be argued that he achieved what was possible in black civil rights. He won the narrowest of election victories in 1960. He needed the support of Southern white Democrats in Congress to support his domestic and foreign policies and so he needed to move cautiously on civil rights. According to his British biographer, Hugh Brogan, in *Kennedy* (1996):

> Kennedy entered the White House at a moment when the issue of racial oppression could no longer be dodged. He had to act, and did so effectively and (in the main) willingly. There is no reason to believe that any other man who could have been elected president in 1960 would have done better and perhaps none could have done so well.

On his inaugural day, Kennedy spotted that the guard of honour of the US Coast Guard contained no African-Americans and so he later pressured the Coast Guard to recruit black people. On deeper investigation, Kennedy found that, in the State Department, only 15 out of 3467 people in the foreign service were African-Americans. Robert F. Kennedy found only 10 out of 995 Justice Department employees to be black. As a result, by Executive Order, JFK created, in March 1961, the President's Committee on Equal Employment Opportunity (PCEEO). Chaired by Vice President Lyndon Johnson, the PCEEO aimed to prevent discrimination for all those doing business with the Federal Government. Given the size of the Federal Government, this involved thousands of employers. Kennedy also forced the Civil Service Commission to appoint more black employees. If it had not been for conservative opposition in Congress, he might well have appointed the first African-American to a Cabinet post – Robert C. Weaver in the Department of Housing and Urban Development. This became reality during Johnson's presidency. In 1961, Secretary for the Interior Stewart Udall was able to persuade the national football team, the Washington Redskins, to end their ban on hiring African-American players.

Finally, Kennedy became the first president to appoint an African-American as a Federal Circuit judge when he appointed NAACP lawyer Thurgood Marshall to the Court of Appeals for the Second Circuit in New York. However, politics is full of compromises. To obtain Southern white support for Marshall's appointment, Kennedy had to agree to the appointment of Harold Cox to the Federal Circuit Court in Mississippi. Cox was a noted white supremacist.

By the time of his assassination, Kennedy had begun to address the noted imbalance of African-Americans in government employment. The PCEEO began the first steps to affirmative action, ensuring that places were set aside for ethnic minorities in companies wishing to gain government contracts. This was called Plans for Progress. Although, in retrospect, this was a modest measure, Kennedy's Civil Rights Bill had been carefully crafted to give black people more rights without alienating the conservative coalition in Congress.

Did Johnson merely fulfil Kennedy's legacy on civil rights?

Did Lyndon Johnson bring about the second Reconstruction?

Between 1963 and 1969 the Jim Crow laws, which had made African-Americans second-class citizens in the Old South, were abolished. This was achieved primarily through three Acts of Congress: the Civil Rights Act 1964, the Voting Rights Act 1965 and the Civil Rights Act 1968. To many contemporaries, this process seemed like a second Reconstruction era. The first Reconstruction era, 1863–77, had seen the abolition of slavery and the granting of full civil and political rights to African-Americans. Following 1877, white supremacy was re-established across the South. Then, from 1963 to 1969, the hopes of the first Reconstruction era were put into practice. Does Lyndon Johnson deserve all the credit in achieving this transformation in American race relations? Doris Kearns Goodwin, an early biographer of LBJ, states in *Lyndon Johnson & the American Dream* (1976):

His position on racial issues was more advanced than that of any other American president: had he done nothing else in his entire

Civil rights legislation passed by Congress 1963–9

Civil Rights Act 1964

- Title I: Introduced tough new controls over state voting laws and included guidelines for the use of literacy tests.
- Title II: Outlawed racial segregation for all public facilities and accommodation.
- Title III: Outlawed racial segregation for all government facilities.
- Title IV: Provided federal assistance for the desegregation of public schools.
- Title V: Expanded the powers of the federal Commission on Civil Rights.
- Title VI: Forbade racial discrimination in any federally assisted programme.
- Title VII: Forbade all discrimination in employment, including race, colour, religion, national origin and sex. (This was an important move towards equality of men and women.)
- Also set up the Equal Employment Opportunities Commission (EEOC) to ensure that the Act was followed.

The Voting Rights Act 1965

- Banned literacy tests for voter registration.
- Appointed federal examiners to ensure that voter registration was fair and legal.

Civil Rights Act 1968

- Outlawed discrimination on the basis of colour, race, religion or national origin in the rental or sale of housing, except in owner-occupied or owner-managed units.
- Outlawed racial discrimination in jury selection.
- Made it a federal crime to interfere with voting, work, schooling and participation in federally assisted programmes.
- Made it illegal to interfere with civil rights workers.
- Introduced fines and imprisonment for anyone who travelled across state lines to foment or participate in a riot.

life, his contributions to civil rights would have earned him a lasting place in the annals of history.

Bruce Miroff, a radical critic of both Kennedy and Johnson, quoted by Steven F. Lawson in *The Johnson Years* (1981), stated:

> No other administration accomplished so much in the way of civil rights legislation; no other president undertook such a commitment to the black cause.

On paper, Johnson's achievements do look very impressive. When he became president on 22 November 1963, JFK's Civil Rights Bill had been held back by the Rules Committee of the House of Representatives. As a tribute to the memory of the murdered President, LBJ used all his persuasive skills to get the Civil Rights Act passed into law by 2 July 1964.

According to historian Kevern Verney, in *Black Civil Rights in America* (2000), 'the Civil Rights Act brought to fruition the Bill introduced by Kennedy in 1963'. In the administrative history of the Justice Department, Kennedy's contribution is seen as significant. Even though the House Rules Committee had delayed the Civil Rights Bill of 1963, Justice Department civil rights lawyers had ensured that when the Bill emerged from the House Judiciary Committee for consideration by the whole House of Representatives it still contained JFK's proposals for strong federal action on civil rights. Johnson was able to ensure a smooth passage through Congress once he became president. His supporters in the Senate broke a 57-day **filibuster** by anti-civil rights senators. Johnson also met with leaders of civil rights groups such as CORE and SNCC who agreed to suspend major demonstrations until after the presidential election of November 1964. LBJ hoped to prevent a white backlash that would have benefited his Republican opponent for the presidency, Barry Goldwater.

In the passage of the Voting Rights Act, Johnson's support for further action has been called into question. According to Professor Stephen F. Lawson, in 'Civil Rights', in *The Johnson Years* (1981):

> Johnson preferred to postpone further legislative action on civil rights, but the resumption of mass protests in Selma, Alabama, in 1965, forced him to change his mind.

Under the leadership of Martin Luther King, African-American civil rights activists had decided to highlight the plight of voter registration problems for black people in the Old South. A civil rights march, from Selma to Montgomery, Alabama, was met with

Filibuster: an attempt to stop legislation being passed by prolonged speaking. If speaking and debate is not completed by the end of a Congressional year a proposal for reform has to be resubmitted the following year. The Senate has complete freedom of speech, so senators have the right to speak on any subject and not necessarily on the topic under consideration.

National Guard: US equivalent of the territorial army. Each state possesses its own National Guard. As Commander in Chief of all US armed forces the president can assume command of any state National Guard by 'federalising' it.

violence by Alabama state police at Pettus Bridge on Sunday 7 March. The media coverage of 'Bloody Sunday' helped force Johnson to federalise the Alabama **National Guard** to protect the marchers. From 17 March to 25 March, over 25 000 civil rights protestors completed the march. During the march, two white civil rights supporters, Viola Liuzzo and Protestant Minister James Reeb were murdered. These events prompted Johnson to convene a joint session of Congress where he announced his intention to introduce a Voting Rights Bill.

The Civil Rights Act 1964 and the Voting Rights Act 1965 effectively brought to an end racial discrimination against African-Americans in public facilities and in voter registration. In his book, *The Vantage Point: Perspectives of the Presidency, 1963–1969* (1971), Lyndon Johnson said:

> With the passage of the Civil Rights Act 1964 and [the Voting Rights Act] 1965, the barriers to freedom began tumbling down. At long last the legal rights of American citizens – the right to vote, to hold a job, to enter a public place, to go to school – were given concrete protection.

Could Johnson have done more?

The Acts did not, however, bring an end to African-American discontent. As the Voting Rights Bill passed through Congress a major race riot occurred in the Watts district of Los Angeles, now known as South Central LA. Between 11 and 15 August 1965, 34 people were killed and over 1000 were injured. Almost 3500 rioters and looters were arrested. According to historian Kevern Verney, in *Black Civil Rights in America* (2000):

> Watts was one of the first of 239 outbreaks of racial violence in over 200 US cities in the five 'long hot summers' from 1964 to 1968. Almost every large American city outside of the South was affected, including Oakland in California in 1965 and 1966, Cleveland, Ohio, 1966 and 1968, Chicago, Illinois, 1966 and 1968, Newark, New Jersey, 1967, and Detroit, Michigan, in 1967. In 1964 there were 16 serious outbreaks of violence in 16 cities, but the first five months of 1968 alone saw 65 riots in 64 cities.

Johnson was both perplexed and angry at inner-city African-American rioting. He stated 'that all that crazy rioting almost ruined everything'. It seemed to him that African-Americans were ungrateful for his efforts in civil rights and inner-city regeneration.

Frightened African-American girls fleeing from police during a riot in Brooklyn, 1964.

It clearly slowed any further plans Johnson had for legislative action. Plans to introduce a further Civil Rights Bill in 1966 were curbed. James Harvey, in *Black Civil Rights During the Johnson Administration* (1973), believed that Johnson did not push the 1966 Bill because 'he was thinking about a growing white backlash'. When the Civil Rights Act 1968 was finally passed, it contained a section that was aimed at rioters and at those who fomented race riots. Such a section had to be included to placate Congressional concerns about the 'long hot summers' of rioting.

Johnson can be criticised for his reaction to the riots. On 29 July 1967, he set up the Kerner Commission to investigate the causes of the rioting. The Commission presented its findings in February 1968. The report regarded white racism as an important contributory factor. It called for sweeping reforms in housing, employment, education and welfare. Johnson ignored its proposals. The costs of such proposals came at a time when the administration was finding it increasingly difficult to fund the Vietnam War.

There was also another problem regarding the Vietnam War and the civil rights movement. Martin Luther King began to attack US policy on Vietnam. On 4 April 1967, Martin Luther King delivered an address at the Riverside Church in New York City. In the speech, he compared American action in Vietnam with Nazi action in the Second World War. He said:

> 'We have destroyed their [the Vietnamese's] two most cherished institutions: the family and the village. We have destroyed their land and crops. We have supported the enemies of the peasants of Saigon [capital of South Vietnam]. We have corrupted their women and children and killed their men. What do you think as we test our latest weapons on them, just as the Germans tested out new medicine and new tortures in the concentration camps of Europe?'

Later in April, King attended the 'Spring mobilisation to end the war in Vietnam'. From 1966, Vietnam was inreasingly coming to dominate Johnson's presidency and so King's anti-war actions hit Johnson's own policy position hard. King also launched the Poor People's Campaign in 1967. He wanted Congress to enact a Bill of Rights for the Disadvantaged. This would involve a massive federally funded programme of aid to the poor. Again, this hit Johnson's policy position hard as it was a direct criticism of his own 'war on poverty'. As a result, the close relationship Martin Luther King had developed with the Johnson White House came to an end.

In addition, as inner-city violence escalated in the North, more militant groups began to represent African-American opinion. In 1966, the Black Panther Party was formed. It adopted a more confrontational and aggressive stance in support of African-American rights. It wanted African-American rights to incorporate social and economic rights as well as civil and political rights.

In the last years of his presidency, Johnson became increasingly remote from the African-American community and has been criticised for not enforcing the civil rights legislation he helped to pass. Historian Allan Wolk, in *The Presidency and Black Civil Rights: Eisenhower to Nixon* (1971), claims that Johnson handed over enforcement to the Justice Department, which was led by the cautious Attorney General Nicholas Katzenbach. Wolk claims that LBJ should have given enforcement to Hubert Humphrey, his vice president, who had briefly acted as civil rights coordinator in the administration and had been very effective.

Even within his own political party, Johnson faced criticism. At the Democratic National Convention, in August 1964, Johnson faced two delegations from Mississippi. On one side, was the all-white, segregationist official delegation. On the other, was a delegation representing the Mississippi Freedom Democratic Party. This had been organised by the SNCC and represented African-Americans. Johnson allowed the official white delegation to represent Mississippi. However, he gave the Freedom Democratic Party two votes at the Convention as a compromise. This angered the official delegation into leaving the Convention.

By 1968, Johnson was soundly condemned by Southern white people. In that year, former Democrat governor of Alabama, George Wallace, ran against the Democrats for the presidency. He formed the American Independent Party. He polled 9.9 million votes and carried five Southern states with a combined Electoral College of 46.

Overall, Johnson was proud of his achievements. He had appointed the first African-American Cabinet member, Robert C. Weaver, and the first African-American US Supreme Court judge, Thurgood Marshall. In December 1972, shortly before his death, Johnson held a conference on civil rights at the Johnson Library in Johnson City, Texas. Several civil rights leaders took part and congratulated him on his efforts. In his own conversations with his biographer Doris Kearns Goodwin, he regarded his record in civil rights to be his greatest achievement.

Assessment

In terms of actual achievement, Johnson clearly did more than Kennedy to aid racial equality. The Civil Rights Act 1964 and the Voting Rights Act 1965 stand out as great legislative achievements. However, in achieving these momentous changes Johnson had a number of advantages. He benefited from the wave of sympathy following Kennedy's assassination. He also built on work carried out during Kennedy's presidency. After all, as vice president, he had chaired the PCEEO. The Civil Rights Act of 1964 was, in essence, Kennedy's Civil Rights Bill of the previous year. Johnson also benefited from a pliant, supportive Congress. The eighty-ninth Congress, elected in 1964, was dominated by Liberal Democrats who supported Johnson's stance on legislative action.

Yet, Johnson clearly deserves praise for the speed and effectiveness of his intervention to aid African-Americans. His command of Congress meant the two landmark Acts of 1964 and 1965 became law. Johnson's 'war on poverty' also aided poor and disadvantaged black people. However, what had begun so promisingly in 1963/4 began to face problems by 1966/7. The increase in inner-city racial violence highlighted the social and economic plight of Northern African-Americans. Also, Johnson's growing preoccupation with the Vietnam War drew him away from domestic problems such as civil rights. In the end, Johnson's triumph was a flawed triumph.

Both Kennedy and Johnson benefited from the dynamism of the civil rights movement. Leaders such as Martin Luther King and organisations such as CORE and SNCC made black civil rights the major domestic issue facing both presidents. In the television era, no president could stand idle when peaceful demonstrators were beaten by police in Southern states such as Mississippi and Alabama. Both JFK and LBJ were placed in a position where they had to confront what sociologist Gunnar Myrdal termed the 'American dilemma' – the issue of race. When confronted, both presidents acted positively to address civil rights.

Who did more for black civil rights: JFK or LBJ?

1. Read the following extract and answer the question.

   'We are confronted primarily by a moral question. It is as old as the Scriptures and is as clear as the American Constitution. The heart of the question is whether all Americans are to be afforded equal rights and equal opportunities: whether they are going to treat our fellow Americans as we want to be treated.

   'We face a moral crisis as a country and a people. It cannot be met by repressive police action. It cannot be left to increased demonstrations in the streets. It cannot be quieted by token moves or talk.'

   (From a nationally televised speech by President John F. Kennedy on 11 June 1963.

   Using information from the extract above, and from this section, explain what Kennedy and Johnson did to give African-Americans equal rights and equal opportunities.

2. 'The Civil Rights Act of 1964 was a turning point in the development of African-American rights during the Kennedy-Johnson years.' How far do you agree with this statement?

3

Who was more responsible for US involvement in Vietnam: JFK or LBJ?

To what extent did Kennedy commit the US to involvement in Vietnam?

Did Johnson merely follow Kennedy's policies on Vietnam?

Framework of events

1954	Geneva Peace Accords; temporary division of French Indo-China into four states
1956	Supported by the US, anti-communist Ngo Dinh Diem becomes leader of South Vietnam
1960	National Liberation Front (NFL) of South Vietnam is born; beginning of communist attempt to overthrow South Vietnam Government
1961	JFK increases number of US military advisers to South Vietnam
1962	International agreement of Laos, which declares that country 'neutral'
	Strategic Hamlets Programme begins
1963	Assassination of Ngo Dinh Diem
	Assassination of Kennedy three weeks later
	LBJ takes over US presidency
1964	Gulf of Tonkin incident and resolution
1965	Operation Rolling Thunder begins
	US ground troops sent to South Vietnam
1968	Communist Tet Offensive in South Vietnam
	US troop level reaches 565 000
	LBJ announces he will not seek re-election as president
	LBJ begins negotiations with North Vietnam

THE Vietnam War bitterly divided the USA in a way no other conflict had done since the Civil War of 1861–5. Over two and a half million Americans served in Vietnam. Fifty-eight thousand were killed. It was the first time in US history that America had lost a war.

Why did the USA become involved in a conflict 10 000 miles from

Indo-China

This map shows Indo-China in 1954, after the Geneva Accords.

- Indo-China is a region of South East Asia, once ruled by France until 1954. Between 1946 and 1954, France fought a major war against Vietnamese nationalists who wanted independence from France. By 1954, France had lost 78 000 people in the war.

- In 1954, in Geneva, Switzerland, an agreement was made between the USA, USSR, China, Britain and France about the future of Indo-China.

- Indo-China was divided into four states. Two states became monarchies: Laos and Cambodia. However, from the late 1950s, communist forces attempted to take over eastern Laos.

- Vietnam was divided into two states. North Vietnam was communist and ruled by **Ho Chi Minh**. South Vietnam was non-communist. It was ruled by **Ngo Dinh Diem**, who acted as a dictator.

- The Geneva Peace Accords (Agreement) planned to have elections throughout Vietnam in 1956 to decide its future. Under US pressure, Diem cancelled the elections. President Eisenhower feared Ho Chi Minh would win and create a united, communist Vietnam.

- In 1960, communists in the South created the NLF, National Liberation Front. The USA called them Viet Cong (VC). They planned a guerrilla war, with Northern assistance, to unite Vietnam as a communist state.

**Ho Chi Minh
(1890–1969)**
Ho Chi Minh was founder
and leader of North Vietnam from 1945 to his
death in 1969. He led the
fight against the French in
1946–54. He was a
communist, who wanted to
unite all the Vietnamese
people into one state. He
supported the fight of the
National Liberation Front,
within South Vietnam, with
arms, equipment and
troops from the North.

**Ngo Dinh Diem
(1901–63)**
Ngo Dinh Diem was ruler
of South Vietnam from 1956 to 1963. He was a
Roman Catholic, corrupt
autocrat, who was bitterly
opposed to communists. He
had also opposed the
French and was seen by
the USA as a Vietnamese
nationalist. His increasing
unpopularity with the
Buddhist majority forced
the USA to organise a
military coup against him
in November 1963.

the USA? Ever since the 1960s, contemporaries and historians have debated who was responsible for US military involvement. Did JFK lay the foundations for involvement? Had JFK lived would the involvement of US ground troops have been avoided? Was it really Lyndon Johnson's war?

Dependent upon whom you believe, Vietnam destroyed the presidencies of both men. The plot of Oliver Stone's film, *JFK*, suggests that Kennedy was assassinated because he wanted to pull out of Vietnam. Johnson's presidency was clearly adversely affected. His decision not to seek re-election as president in 1968 was directly due to Vietnam.

To what extent did Kennedy commit the US to involvement in Vietnam?

Kennedy and Indo-China in 1961

In his inaugural address as US president, made on 20 January 1961, JFK stated:

> 'Let every nation know … that we shall pay any price, bear any burden, meet any hardship, support any friend, oppose any foe, in order to assure the survival and success of liberty.'

To understand JFK's view towards Vietnam one must remember that he became president at the height of the Cold War. It was widely believed by decision makers in Washington DC at the time that the USA faced a communist conspiracy to extend communism across the globe. In this endeavour, the USSR, Communist China and North Vietnam all acted together. Opposing communism in Indo-China was part of a worldwide conflict.

The importance of the USA in the global conflict against communism was made clear by the outgoing President Dwight Eisenhower. In 1954, Eisenhower had stated:

> 'You have a row of dominoes set up, you knock over the first one, and what will happen to the last one is the certainty that it will go over very quickly ... When we come to a possible sequence of events, the loss of Indo-China, of Burma [Myanmar], of Thailand, of Malaya and Indonesia following.'

In addition, when Eisenhower briefed Kennedy on foreign policy in 1961, he stated that the most important issue facing the USA in the conflict with communism at that time was the communist attempt to take over Laos. In fact, for most of his presidency, Kennedy spent more time dealing with Laos than South Vietnam. It was only in 1963 that Vietnam became a more dominant problem.

The case against holding Kennedy responsible for US military involvement in Vietnam

Ever since JFK's assassination, speculation has developed about exactly what he was willing to do to protect South Vietnam from a communist takeover.

Robert F. Kennedy, JFK's younger brother, who was attorney general between 1961 and 1963, said in a conversation in 1967:

> 'We saw the position the French were in [in 1954] and my brother was determined early that we would never get into that position.'

General Maxwell Taylor, who led several US missions to South Vietnam between 1961 and 1963, made a similar comment regarding JFK. After Taylor requested that the USA send 8000 ground troops to aid South Vietnam in 1961, he stated:

> 'I don't recall anyone strongly against this plan except one man,

General Maxwell Taylor (1901–87)
Taylor was a Second-World-War general who led the 101st Airborne Brigade at the Battle of Arnhem. Between 1961 and 1965, he was a personal military adviser on Vietnam. He made several fact-finding missions to South Vietnam to appraise the situation. In the autumn of 1961, Taylor, with economic adviser Walt Rostow, visited Saigon and reported on the chaotic situation in South Vietnam. Taylor suggested sending ground troops. His wish was finally granted by LBJ in March 1965.

the President. It was really the President's personal conviction that US ground troops shouldn't go in.'

Some historians also believe that JFK was unwilling to make a large military commitment. Arthur M. Schlesinger, in *Robert Kennedy and His Times* (1978), believes JFK occupied a middle position between two opposing groups of advisers on Vietnam. On the one hand, there were 'hawks' such as the head of the **Joint Chiefs of Staff**, General Lyman Lemnitzer. He wanted strong military support for South Vietnam. On the other hand, there were those like US Ambassador to India J.K. Galbraith, who wanted a phased withdrawal of US support for Vietnam. This group tended to support a solution similar to that achieved over Laos in 1962. In that year US envoy, William Averell Harriman, was able to get an agreement with the USSR. Both sides agreed on the 'neutralisation' of Laos. This meant the creation of a coalition government that contained communist and non-communist elements. According to Arthur Schlesinger, Kennedy wanted a solution to the problem in South Vietnam that would avoid a large military commitment by the USA. He wanted to support the South Vietnamese Government in defeating the communist guerrillas.

Joint Chiefs of Staff: the leading generals and admirals of the US armed forces.

On JFK's accession to presidency, there were 800 military advisers in South Vietnam. He increased this number to 3000 by December 1961, to 10 000 in 1962 and to 16 000 by the time of his assassination. Advisers included a contingent of Green Berets – an elite group of special forces trained to fight guerrilla war. JFK hoped that such forces could help defeat communism in **Third World** countries while avoiding a direct military confrontation with the USSR. In addition, JFK increased military aid to the South Vietnamese army (ARVN). In many ways, JFK was buying time. In 1961 and 1962, Vietnam was still a sideshow in US foreign policy. Crises over Berlin and Cuba absorbed much more attention.

Third World: a term used during the Cold War. The First World was the West, including the USA, Japan and Western Europe; the Second World was the communist world. The rest of the globe was termed the Third World. It included Southern Asia, Africa and Latin America.

According to historian Lawrence Freedman in his book *Kennedy's Wars* (2000), JFK planned to withdraw US advisers once he had won the 1964 presidential election. Senator Mike Mansfield remembers JFK saying, 'I can't depart until 1965 – after I'm re-elected.' When asked by his aide Ken O'Donnell how the USA would be able to withdraw from South Vietnam, JFK stated, 'Easy, put a government in there that will ask us to leave.'

Throughout 1961 and 1962, the Kennedy administration consistently stated that Ngo Dinh Diem was the strong man of Vietnam, who had to be supported in order to defeat the communist uprising. However, by 1963, Diem's regime had become very unpopular. He was a Roman Catholic in charge of a predominantly Buddhist country. His government was dominated by Catholics and was noted for corruption. Instead of using US aid to fight the communists, he used it to gain support for his own government.

Strategic Hamlets Programme: villagers in rural areas were rounded up and put in hamlets to isolate them from communist influences.

In 1962, the US suggested the creation of the **Strategic Hamlets Programme**. A similar programme had been used by the British in Malaya, where they successfully defeated a communist uprising in the 1950s. However, Diem and his brother Ngo Dinh Nhu did not create hamlets in areas threatened by communists but in areas where they could gain more political support. They believed the USA would always back them, no matter what they did, because the alternative was a communist victory.

By the spring of 1963, JFK's advisers were suggesting that Diem was in fact the cause of growing communist influence rather than the solution.

In November 1963, generals of ARVN, with CIA help, overthrew Diem, killing him and his brother in the process. This was part of JFK's plan to find a strong South Vietnamese Government that would allow the US to eventually withdraw.

In assessing what JFK might have done had he lived beyond 22 November 1963, several historians have passed comment. Lawrence Freedman, in *Kennedy's Wars* (2000), believes that JFK's advisers were badly divided about what to do in South Vietnam and that Kennedy's policy was aimed at healing rifts among them. Hugh Brogan, in *Kennedy* (1996), states:

> All that can be said is that Kennedy would have been more reluctant than Johnson in accepting a [military commitment] and might well have looked sooner, harder and more successfully for an alternative.

In *The Imperial Presidency* (1973), Arthur Schlesinger helps to explain why. In sending 16 000 advisers, JFK had merely followed actions taken by previous presidents in foreign policy. Also, by November 1963, only 100 US servicemen had been killed in South Vietnam. To most Americans, Vietnam was still a little-known sideshow.

The case for holding Kennedy responsible for US involvement in Vietnam

JFK fervently believed that the US faced a global communist threat. He accepted Eisenhower's 'domino theory'. JFK was faced with a communist uprising in a 'friendly country' and could not afford defeat. US prestige across the world was at stake. Only in this global context can JFK's actions be understood.

Even in 'neutral' Laos, JFK used the CIA to support anti-communist forces. Supplies were flown in, by CIA-owned 'Air America', from Thailand. In addition, US B52 bombers attacked communist positions in central and eastern Laos between 1962 and 1963. These actions were done secretly without Congressional approval.

Kennedy was determined to use South Vietnam as a testing ground for new theories on how to combat communist aggression. He placed great hope in counter-insurgency forces, which would fight guerrilla forces on their own terms. The Green Berets were the force that would be used across the globe for this purpose. According to historian Stephen E. Ambrose, in *Rise to Globalism: American Foreign Policy Since 1938* (1971), 'Kennedy was prepared to do anything to prevent a Viet Cong victory.'

The main strategy of the Kennedy administration until 1963 was to support Ngo Dinh Diem at all costs. He was believed to be the strong man, capable of defeating communism. Unfortunately, such a policy backfired. Diem was immensely unpopular. His leadership was in many ways the reason why the Viet Cong (VC) gained influence in 1961 and 1962. Diem feared a military coup against him by ARVN generals and was very suspicious of any general who won military victories. Instead of fighting the VC, ARVN generals tried to avoid conflict at all costs. A spectacular example was the Battle of Ap Bac in January 1963 when 2000 ARVN troops with US helicopter support were ordered not to move forward and attack 350 lightly armed VC. Instead they were ordered to change their mission to one of blocking positions – a decision that had serious consequences.

Within the USA, opposition to Diem's regime came from journalists such as Neil Sheehan of *United Press International* and David Halberstam of *The New York Times*. The latter noted:

> [Diem] became more convinced than ever that it had its ally [USA] in a corner, that it could do anything it wanted, that continued support would be guaranteed because of the communist threat [and that] the US could not suddenly admit that it had made a vast mistake.

It was Halberstam who first put forward the 'quagmire theory' – the idea that the USA, without forethought, had been sucked into giving military support to Diem.

A key turning point came in August 1963 with the appointment

JFK/LBJ advisers on Vietnam

The title 'The best and the brightest' was given to the members of the JFK/LBJ administrations because they were recruited from top universities and large businesses.

Dean Rusk: Secretary of State
- Rusk was a highly intelligent man, who had studied for three years at Oxford University before joining the State Department during President Truman's administration (1945–53).
- He was former Under Secretary of State whom JFK chose because he thought he would be a good second-in-command. JFK wanted to be his own Secretary of State. During the Kennedy years, Rusk was sidelined as JFK tended to get advice from his brother, Robert F. Kennedy. Rusk was given more freedom to operate under LBJ, but he was never in the position where he could have offered independent advice. In the debates on Vietnam, he was overshadowed first by Robert Kennedy and later by McGeorge Bundy.

Robert McNamara: Secretary of Defense
- McNamara had attended the University of California at Berkeley and also Harvard University. After one month as chief executive of the Ford Motor Company, he left his post, in January 1961, to become Defense Secretary. He became JFK's and LBJ's major adviser on Vietnam.
- With a razor-sharp mind and strong personality, McNamara became a central figure in developing US policy on Vietnam. Kept in the post by Johnson, he virtually ran US policy on Vietnam until August 1968 when he resigned to become president of the World Bank. He was described as aggressive and as being characterised by toughness, quickness, fluency, competence, incorruptibility and a force of personality.

McGeorge Bundy: National Security Adviser
- Bundy came from a very wealthy family in Boston, Massachusetts. He attended the best private schools: the Dexter School (where JFK also attended) and Groton (where Franklin D. Roosevelt had been a pupil). He then studied at Yale University. At 30 years old, he became a lecturer in Government at Harvard University.
- Although Bundy was a supporter of the Republican Party, he was strongly attracted to JFK's policies and willing to join his government. He was appointed National Security Adviser from 1961 to 1966, when he resigned to become president of the Ford Foundation. As National Security Adviser, he usually worked a 12-hour day and played a central role in all JFK's foreign policy decisions over Berlin, Cuba and Vietnam. His brother, William P. Bundy, Assistant Secretary of State for Far Eastern Affairs, led the Working Group in 1965 that advised LBJ to begin bombing North Vietnam.

of Henry Cabot Lodge as US Ambassador to South Vietnam. Lodge had been defeated by JFK in the Senate election of 1952. He had also been Nixon's vice-presidential candidate in 1960. From the moment Lodge arrived in Saigon, on 22 August 1963, he was convinced Diem had to be removed. Nationwide protests by Buddhists had brought the country to the point of revolt. From late August to November, Lodge worked with ARVN generals to remove Diem. On 1 November 1963, Diem was overthrown.

Diem's fall, however, led to increased instability in the Southern Government. Diem was first replaced by General Minh and then, in February 1964, by General Khahn. They both formed weak governments. Instead of improving the situation, JFK's policy had made matters worse.

When JFK was assassinated three weeks later, his Vietnam policy was in a mess. Although JFK had ruled out military action against North Vietnam in 1963, Lawrence Freedman in *Kennedy's Wars* (2000) suggests that, in 1964, he might have been forced to change his mind as the military situation deteriorated in the South. This is also the view held by several of today's historians. Historian William H. Chafe notes, in *The Unfinished Journey: America Since World War II* (1999):

> Kennedy and his advisers had charted a course that step-by-step involved the United States inextricably deeper in the Vietnam tragedy. As Ambassador Maxwell Taylor later recalled, 'Diem's overthrow set in motion a sequence of crises, political and military, over the next two years which eventually forced President Johnson in 1965 to choose between accepting defeat or introducing US combat troops.'

Historian James N. Giglio states, in *The Presidency of John F. Kennedy* (1991):

> Given what we know of President Kennedy, it is difficult to conceive of his pulling out of Vietnam without a reasonable honourable settlement.

So was Lyndon Johnson put in an impossible position over Vietnam when he became president on 22 November 1963?

Did Johnson merely follow Kennedy's policies on Vietnam?

When LBJ became president he did possess some knowledge of Vietnam. As vice president, he had visited South Vietnam during a tour of Asia. However, the situation was still regarded as a sideshow in the early months of Johnson's presidency and he concentrated on enacting domestic reform such as the Civil Rights Act and the Great Society Programme.

Nevertheless, it was difficult for LBJ to change Kennedy's policies on Vietnam. He had, after all, inherited Kennedy's foreign policy advisers. On 26 November 1963, a National Security Action Memorandum (NSAM) stated:

> The central object of the US to South Vietnam [is] to assist the people and government of that country to win their contest against the externally directed and supported communist conspiracy.

So, from November 1963 to the summer of 1964, US policy followed the line of offering financial and military aid to the South Vietnamese Government. Johnson openly stated that he would carry on JFK's work. He said:

> 'I swore to myself that I would carry on. When I took over I often felt as if President Kennedy was sitting in the room looking at me.'

However, by the time Johnson decided not to seek re-election, on 31 March 1968, the situation was transformed. There were 565 000 US ground troops stationed in South Vietnam. The US air force flew bombing missions against targets in North Vietnam. General Westmoreland, US commander in Vietnam, was requesting 200 000 extra troops. The war was costing the US $60 million a day and the USA was bitterly divided about supporting a war that had cost over 35 000 lives and wounded 175 000.

There is considerable evidence to suggest that LBJ would commit the USA to a major war in Vietnam. Historian William H. Chafe, in *The Unfinished Journey: America Since World War II* (1999), suggests that Johnson's Texan background made him determined not to be the first president to lose a war.

By mid-1964, the military and political situation in South Vietnam had deteriorated so much that LBJ's advisers feared the state might collapse. The USA could not afford to lose South Vietnam to communism at the height of the Cold War.

Like JFK, Johnson was a firm believer in the 'domino theory' and the need to stand up to communist aggression. On 27 April 1965, he made the comment:

'We are resisting aggression, and as long as aggressors attack, we shall stay there [Vietnam] and resist them – whether we make friends or lose friends.'

Yet, as late as 12 August 1964, Johnson was telling the American Bar Association:

'They [the South Vietnamese] call upon us to supply American boys to do the job that Asian boys should do. They ask us to take reckless actions which might risk the lives of millions. Moreover, such action would offer no solution at all to the real problems of Vietnam.'

Why did Johnson decide to escalate the war, between February 1964 and March 1965?

There are a number of differing interpretations as to why Johnson decided to escalate the war. One interpretation involves the presidential election of 1964 when Johnson faced an extreme anti-communist opponent in the Republican candidate Barry Goldwater.

At the height of the campaign, between 2 August and 4 August, an incident occurred in the Gulf of Tonkin, off the coast of North Vietnam. On 2 August, two US destroyers, the USS Maddox and the USS C. Turner Joy were allegedly attacked by North Vietnamese torpedo boats. A second, alleged attack occurred on 4 August. There is considerable confusion even today about what actually happened. In the confidential Department of Defense documents, the Pentagon Papers, released in 1971 (see **Landmark Study** below), there is a strong suggestion that no actual attacks took place. Johnson,

Landmark Study   The documents that changed people's views

The Pentagon Papers, 1971

These were government documents on the Vietnam War, compiled under the instruction of Secretary of Defense Robert McNamara. They contained records from the State and Defense Departments and from CIA files. They also contained papers prepared for the Joint Chiefs of Staff and communications between the State Department and the US Embassy in Saigon. The documents go as far back as 1945, but have detailed coverage of the 1963–5 period.

The papers were released to *The New York Times* by Defense Department employee Dr Daniel Ellsberg. President Nixon tried to prevent their publication and took his case to the US Supreme Court but lost. He also tried to discredit Ellsberg by attempting to steal his personal records from his psychiatrist.

The Pentagon Papers revealed the depth of secret activity undertaken by the US Government in South East Asia. In particular, they highlighted the deception surrounding the Gulf of Tonkin Resolution.

however, used the incident to intervene directly in the Vietnam War. For most of the period since 1963, Secretary of Defense Robert McNamara had run the war. Johnson used the incident to get Congress to pass the South East Asia (or Gulf of Tonkin) Resolution. As historian Arthur M. Schlesinger notes, in *The Imperial Presidency* (1973), this was 'rushed through Congress in a stampede of misinformation and misconception, if not of deliberate deception'. Schlesinger and others such as journalist Neil Sheehan, whose book on Vietnam is called *A Bright Shining Lie: John Paul Vann and America in Vietnam* (1989), see Johnson as deliberately misleading Congress and the US public into escalating the war in Vietnam.

The Gulf of Tonkin Resolution gave the US President powers to wage limited war abroad. Initially, Johnson authorised air attacks against specific targets in North Vietnam. In February 1965, this policy was broadened into Operation Rolling Thunder. This was a systematic attempt to bomb North Vietnam and supply lines through Laos known as the Ho Chi Minh trail. Some historians believe that this was the turning point. Rowland Evans and Robert Novak state in their book *Lyndon Johnson and the Exercise of Power* (1966):

> From that moment the war that had been impersonal, distant and secondary became for Lyndon Johnson the consuming passion of his presidency. It became, more than any other war in the 20th century for any other president, a personal war.

On 8 March 1965, following a Viet Cong attack on a US air base at Pleiku, South Vietnam, Johnson committed ground troops for the first time. Three and a half thousand US Marines landed at Da Nang. By April, the numbers had risen to 18 000. On 28 July 1965, Johnson announced that troop levels would rise to 125 000. They had reached 200 000 by the end of the year.

Should Johnson be blamed personally for direct US military involvement?

To an extent, LBJ was a victim of circumstance. In his biography of Johnson, entitled *Big Daddy from the Pedernales* (1986), historian Paul K. Conkin notes:

> Johnson's policies flowed consistently from a series of decisions made by three earlier presidents [Truman, Eisenhower, Kennedy]. Continuity, not new departures, marked his choices, not because of a lack of experience on his part but because of his own belief and values. He wanted above all else to contain the Vietnam conflict.

It must be remembered that it took LBJ 18 months before he eventually committed ground troops to South Vietnam. In the period from November 1963 to March 1965, considerable debate took place among his advisers about what to do. Throughout this critical period, Johnson received pessimistic reports about the quality of ARVN and its inability to prevent communist infiltration of South Vietnam.

Johnson set up a Working Group to study possible options in South Vietnam. It was chaired by McGeorge Bundy's brother, William P. Bundy, and contained members from the Department of Defense, the Central Intelligence Agency, the State Department and the Joint Chiefs of Staff. William Bundy reported the findings of the Working Group to LBJ. He explained that the South Vietnamese Government was very weak. He advocated bombing the North as a way of taking pressure off the South Vietnamese Government. In 'The War in Vietnam' in *The Johnson Years* (1981), historian George C. Herring notes:

Defense Secretary Robert McNamara and President Johnson after receiving information of new problems in Vietnam in 1964.

The United States [was] primarily responsible for escalating the war [as a] desperate attempt to stave off the collapse of South Vietnam from within.

What Johnson and his major advisers failed to comprehend was the limited impact superior US military technology would have on an enemy determined to unite their own country.

The only dissenting voice from among the inner circle of advisers came from Under Secretary of State George Ball. He thought the commitment of US ground troops would be disastrous. He concluded that once the US was committed to militarily defending South Vietnam they were there for the long haul. His suggestion that up to 500 000 troops would have to be deployed was met with astonishment by the other advisers. However, historians Leslie K. Gelb and Richard H. Betts, in *The Irony of Vietnam: The System Worked* (1979), claim that LBJ and his advisers knew exactly what they were getting into when they escalated the war in February and March 1965.

In retrospect, it is perhaps easy to see the folly of the decision of Johnson and his advisers. However, as historian George Herring states, in 'The War in Vietnam', in *The Johnson Years* (1981):

> It must be stressed that the situation he inherited in Vietnam lent itself to no easy solution – perhaps no solution at all. Those who argue that a more decisive use of military power and a deeper commitment to negotiations would have brought the desired results conveniently overlook the harsh realities of the conflict: (1) a determined, fanatical enemy (2) the threat of Soviet and Chinese intervention (3) a weak ally (4) domestic consensus which wanted success in Vietnam without paying a high price.

Johnson and his administration are often criticised for having made crucial decisions on escalation without notifying Congress. The escalation into a major conflict, involving US troops, was done in an atmosphere of misinformation about what was actually happening. Only after the publication of the Pentagon Papers in 1971, did the degree of deception and misinformation become apparent. On this point, LBJ and his advisers should be held accountable.

Who was responsible?

Whether you believe the US stumbled into the quagmire of a land war in Vietnam or consciously and deliberately chose to do so depends upon the historical evidence available. However, the context of the 1960s needs to be taken into consideration when making your final decision. The USA was involved in a global struggle against communism. It was widely believed that Ho Chi

American soldiers fighting a guerrilla attack on a US artillery-infantry base, 1967.

Minh in Hanoi worked closely with Chairman Mao in China and the Soviet leadership. Any failure to stand up to communism in Vietnam would have worldwide consequences. The USA had already stood up to communist aggression in Europe in the late 1940s over Berlin. It had also done so in Asia in the Korean War. The war in Vietnam was a continuation of the same policy.

The arrogance of American power at the time also needs to be borne in mind. The USA, with its vastly superior military equipment, thought it could easily defeat an economically backward South East Asian state in North Vietnam. The USA greatly under-estimated the nature of guerrilla warfare where lightly-armed troops could be very effective against US forces.

If US military involvement had been kept to aerial bombing, public opinion may have supported the war longer. By committing **conscript** ground troops, the loss of American lives in Vietnam helped turn public opinion against the war by early 1968.

Conscript: a person forced to do compulsory military service.

President Johnson later assessed what had gone wrong. Historian Vaughn Davis Bornet, in *The Presidency of Lyndon B. Johnson* (1983), notes:

> President Johnson admitted that two 'key mistakes' had been made on Vietnam. 'Kennedy should have had more than 16 000 military advisers there in the early 1960s. And then I made the situation worse by waiting 18 months before putting more men in. By then the war was lost.'

This would suggest that, rather than showing reluctance in going to war, Johnson believed that more effective military action earlier would have succeeded.

Who was more responsible for US involvement in Vietnam: JFK or LBJ?

1. Read the following extract and answer the question.

   > *'Johnson and his advisers insisted that by intervening in Vietnam they were defending vital interests of the United States. It resurrected the "domino theory" first publicised by Eisenhower in 1954, warning that the fall of South Vietnam would cause the loss of all South East Asia with disastrous economic, political, and strategic consequences for the United States. Johnson and his Secretary of State, Dean Rusk, repeatedly emphasised that the failure to stand up to aggression would encourage further aggression, upsetting the international order the United States had established since World War II and perhaps provoking a third world war.'*

   (Adapted from G.C. Herring, 'The War in Vietnam', in *The Johnson Years: Foreign Policy, the Great Society, and the White House*, edited by Robert A. Divine, University of Texas Press, 1981, p 28.)

   Using the information in the extract above, and from this section, explain why the USA increased its military commitment in Vietnam between 1961 and 1965.

2. 'Johnson, not Kennedy, was responsible for US military involvement in Vietnam by 1965.' How far do you agree with this statement?

JFK & LBJ: an assessment

JFK

Domestic reform
John F. Kennedy's presidency offered much but delivered little. His New Frontier Programme promised help for the poor and the marginalised. By the time of his assassination, most of the promise lay unfulfilled.

African-American civil rights
Kennedy's approach to African-American civil rights was primarily reactive. During his presidency, African-American activist groups such as CORE, SNCC and SCLC ensured that civil rights became a dominant issue. With a very mixed track record on civil rights before 1961, JFK experienced a steep learning curve as he battled with the effects of 'freedom rides', demonstrations and university entrance problems. By 1963, Kennedy had come to the conclusion that the great issue of race could not be ignored any longer. His Civil Rights Bill of 1963 planned to provide African-Americans with federal enforcement in their quest for equality.

Involvement in Vietnam
JFK inherited a precarious military and political situation in Indo-China. His great triumph was neutralising Laos but even that was a stop-gap arrangement to prevent further communist influence in South East Asia. In South Vietnam, his policy of toppling Ngo Dinh Diem made a bad situation worse. By the time of his assassination, South Vietnam was on the verge of political collapse. Kennedy left Johnson with a very difficult problem from which he found it almost impossible to extricate himself.

LBJ

Domestic reform
Johnson's presidency was one of the greatest in the 20th century in the area of domestic reform. Between 1963 and 1969 and, in particular during the eighty-ninth Congress of 1965/6, almost every area of domestic activity was reformed: education, health care, the environment, inner-city regeneration and consumer protection. The scale of effort and range of reform were truly 'great' in the Great Society Programme.

African-American civil rights
Perhaps, Johnson's greatest presidential triumph was in civil rights. Building on preparatory work by Kennedy, Johnson brought to an end legal discrimination against African-Americans. At the time of his death, in 1973, Johnson felt extremely proud of his achievements in this field. However, in spite of Johnson's triumph, black radicalism and racial conflict increased during his presidency. Although African-Americans had achieved civil and political equality, they were far from achieving social and economic equality with white civilians.

Involvement in Vietnam
If civil rights was Johnson's greatest triumph, Vietnam was his greatest tragedy. By 1968, 565 000 US troops were stationed in South Vietnam. In a war, which seemed to have no end, Johnson decided on 31 March 1968 not to seek re-election as president. When Johnson stood down as president in January 1969, the USA was sharply divided on the Vietnam War in a way not seen since the Civil War of 1861–5. Johnson might be described as the most successful US president of the 20th century for his presidency during 1963–6, but by 1969 he was a broken man.

Further reading

Texts specifically designed for students

Blum, J.M. *Years of Discord: American Politics and Society, 1961–1974* (W.W. Norton and Company, 1991)

Brogan, H. *Kennedy* (Addison-Wesley, 1996)

Chafe, W.H. *The Unfinished Journey: America Since World War II* (Oxford University Press, 1999 (fourth edition))

Cooper, K., Murphy D. and Waldron M. *The United States 1776–1992* (Collins Educational, 2001)

Texts for more advanced study

Bornet, V.D. *The Presidency of Lyndon B. Johnson* (University Press of Kansas, 1983) offers a comprehensive coverage of the New Frontier, civil rights and Vietnam.

Conkin, P.K. *Big Daddy from the Pedernales: Lyndon Baines Johnson* (Twayne Publishers, 1986) contains very good coverage of the Great Society, civil rights and Vietnam.

Dallek, R. *Flawed Giant: Lyndon Johnson and His Times, 1961–1963* (Oxford University Press, 1998) is the sequel to *Lone Star Rising* and the second part of a definitive biography of Johnson.

Giglio, J.N. *The Presidency of John F. Kennedy* (University Press of Kansas, 1991) provides an objective assessment of the Kennedy years.

Heath J.F. *Decade of Disillusionment: The Kennedy-Johnson Years* (Indiana University Press, 1975) offers a critical overview of the whole Kennedy-Johnson period.

Schlesinger, A.M. *Robert Kennedy and His Times* (Andre Deutsch, 1978) offers great insight into both the Kennedy and Johnson presidencies.

Index